CONTENTS

D1711271

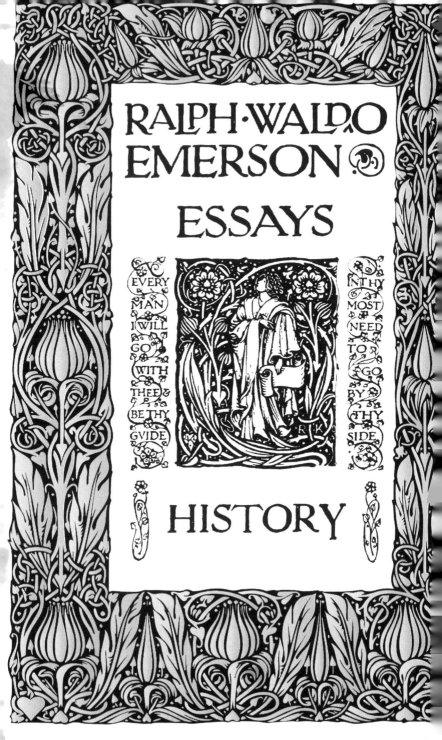

RALPH·WALDO EMERSON

ESSAYS

EVERY MAN I WILL GO WITH THEE & BE THY GVIDE

IN THY MOST NEED TO GO BY THY SIDE

HISTORY

HISTORY

There is no great and no small
To the soul that maketh all :
And where it cometh, all things are ;
And it cometh every where.

I am owner of the sphere,
Of the seven stars and the solar year,
Of Cæsar's hand, and Plato's brain,
Of Lord Christ's heart, and Shakespeare's strain.

Edited by A.D Hendry
Cover Art by A.D Hendry

There is one mind common to all individual men. Every man is an inlet to the same and to all of the same. He that is once admitted to the right of reason is made a freeman of the whole estate. What Plato has thought, he may think ; what a saint has felt, he may feel ; what at any time has befallen any man, he can understand. Who hath access to this universal mind, is a party to all that is or can be done, for this is the only and sovereign agent.

Of the works of this mind history is the record. Its genius is illustrated by the entire series of days. Man is explicable by nothing less than all his history. Without hurry, without rest, the human spirit goes forth from the beginning to embody every faculty, every thought, every emotion, which belongs to it, in appropriate events. But always the thought is prior to the fact ; all the facts of history pre-exist in the mind as laws. Each law in turn is made by circumstances predominant, and the limits of nature give power to but one at a time. A man is the whole encyclopaedia of facts. The creation of a thousand forests is in one acorn ; and Egypt, Greece, Rome, Gaul, Britain, America, lie folded already in the first man. Epoch after epoch, camp, kingdom, empire, republic, democracy, are merely the application of this manifold spirit to the manifold world.

This human mind wrote history, and this must read it. The Sphinx must solve her own riddle. If the whole of history is in one man, it is all to be explained from individual experience. There is a relation between the hours of our life and the centuries of time. As the air I breathe is drawn from the great repositories of nature, as the light on my book is yielded by a star a hundred millions of miles distant, as the poise of my body depends on the equilibrium of centrifugal and centripetal forces, so the hours should be instructed by the ages, and the ages explained by the hours. Of the universal mind each individual man is one more incarnation. All its properties consist in him. Every step in his private experience flashes a light on what great bodies of men have done, and the crises of his life refer to national crises. Every revolution was first a thought in one man's mind ; and when the same thought occurs to another man, it is the key to that era. Every reform was once a private opinion ; and when it shall be a private opinion again, it will solve the problem of the age. The fact narrated must correspond to something in me to be credible or intelligible. We as we read must become Greeks, Romans, Turks, priest and king, martyr and executioner, must fasten these images to some reality in our secret experience, or we shall see nothing, learn nothing. What befel Asdrubal or Cæsar Borgia is as much an illustration of the mind's powers and depravations as what has befallen us. Each new law and political movement has meaning for you. Stand before each of its tablets and say, " Here is one of my coverings. Under this fantastic, or odious, or graceful mask did my Proteus nature hide itself. " This remedies the defect of our too great nearness to ourselves. This throws our own actions into perspective : and as crabs, goats, scorpions, the balance and the waterpot, lose all their meanness when hung as signs in the zodiac, so I can see my own vices without heat in the distant persons of Solomon, Alcibiades, and Catiline.

It is this universal nature which gives worth to particular men and things. Human life as containing this is mysterious and inviolable, and we hedge it round with penalties and laws. All laws derive hence their ultimate reason, all express at last reverence for some command of this supreme illimitable essence. Property also holds of the soul, covers great spiritual facts, and instinctively we at first hold to it with swords and laws, and wide and complex combinations. The obscure consciousness of this fact is the light of all our day, the claim of claims ; the plea for education, for justice, for charity, the foundation of friendship and love, and of the heroism and grandeur which belongs to acts of self-reliance. It is remarkable that involuntarily we always read as superior beings. Universal history, the poets, the romancers, do not in their stateliest pictures,—in the sacerdotal, the imperial palaces, in the triumphs of will, or of genius, any where lose our ear, any where make us feel that we intrude, that this is for our betters ; but rather is it true, that in their grandest strokes, there we feel most at home. All that Shakespeare says of the king, yonder slip of boy that reads in the corner feels that it is true of himself. We sympathise in the great moments of history, in the great discoveries, the great resistances, the great properties, of men ;—because there law was enacted, the sea was searched, the land was found, or the blow was struck *for us*, as we ourselves in that place would have done or applauded.

So it is in respect to tradition and character. We honour the rich, because they have externally the freedom, power, and grace which we feel to be proper to man, proper to us. So all this is said of the wise man by stoic, or oriental or modern essayist, describes to each man his own idea, describes his unattained but attainable self. All literature writes the character of the wise man. All books, monuments, pictures, conversation, are portraits in which the wise man finds the lineaments he is forming. The silent and the loud praise him, and accost him, and he is stimulated wherever he moves as by personal allusions. A wise and good soul, therefore, never needs look for allusions personal and laudatory in discourse. He hears the commendation, not of himself, but more sweet, of that character he seeks, in every word that is said concerning character, yea, further, in every fact that befalls,—in the running river and the rustling corn. Praise is looked, homage tendered, love flows from mute nature, from the mountains and the lights of the firmament.

These hints, dropped as it were from sleep and night, let us use in broad day. The student is to read history actively and not passively ; to esteem his own life the text, and books the commentary. Thus compelled, the muse of history will utter oracles, as never to those who do not respect themselves. I have no expectation that any man will read history alright, who thinks that what was done in a remote age, by men whose names have resounded far, has any deeper sense than what he is doing to-day.

The world exists for the education of each man. There is no age or state or society, or mode of action in history, to which there is not somewhat corresponding in his life. Every thing tends in a most wonderful manner to abbreviate itself and yield its own virtue to him. He should see that he can live all history in his own person. He must sit at home with might and main, and not suffer himself to be bullied by kings or empires, and know that he is greater than all the geography and all the government of the world ; he must transfer the point of view from which history is commonly read, from Rome and Athens and London to himself, and not deny his conviction that he is the Court, and if England or Egypt have any thing to say to him, he will try the case ; if not, let them forever be silent. He must attain and maintain that lofty sight where facts yield their secret sense, and poetry and annals alike. The instinct of the mind, the purpose of nature betrays itself in the use we make of the signal narrations of history. Time dissipates to shining ether the solid angularity of facts. No anchor, no cable, no fences avail to keep a fact a fact. Babylon and Troy and Tyre, an even early Rome, are passing already into fiction. The Garden of Eden, the Sun standing still in Gibeon, is poetry thenceforward to all nations. Who cares what the fact was, when we have thus made a constellation of it to hang in heaven an immortal sign ? London and Paris and New York must go the same way. " What is history, " said Napoleon, " but a fable agreed upon ? " This life of ours is stuck round with Egypt, Greece, Gaul, England, War, colonisation, Church, Court, and Commerce, as with so many flowers and wild ornaments grave and gay. I will not make more account of them. I believe in Eternity. I can find Greece, Palestine, Italy, Spain, and the Islands,—the genius and creative principle of each and of all eras in my own mind.

We are always coming up with the facts that have moved us in history in our private experience, and verifying them here. All history becomes subjective ; in other words, there is properly no History ; only Biography. Every soul must know the whole lesson for itself—must go over the whole ground. What it does not see, what it does not live, it will not know. What the former age has epitomised into a formula or rule for manipular convenience, it will lose all the good of verifying for itself, by means of the wall of that rule. Somewhere or other, some time or other, it will demand and find compensation for that loss by doing the work itself. Ferguson discovered many things in astronomy which had long been known. The better for him.

History must be this, or it is nothing. Every law which the state enacts indicates a fact in human nature ; that is all. We must in our own nature see the necessary reason of every fact,—see how it could and must be. So stand before every public, every private work ; before an oration of Burke, before a victory of Napoleon, before a martyrdom of Sir Thomas More, of Sidney, of Marmaduke Robinson, before a French Reign of Terror, and a Salem hanging of witches, before a fanatic Revival, and the Animal Magnetism in Paris, or in providence. We assume that we under like influence should be alike affected, and should achieve the like ; and we aim to master intellectually the steps, and reach the same height or the same degradation that our fellow, our proxy has done.

All inquiry into antiquity,—all curiosity respecting the pyramids, the excavated cities, Stonehenge, the Ohio Circles, Mexico, Memphis, is the desire to do away this wild, savage, and preposterous There or Then, and produce in its place the Here and Now. It is to banish the *Not me,* and supply the *Me.* It is to abolish difference, and restore unity. Belzoni digs and measure in the mummy-pits and pyramids of Thebes, until he can see the end of the difference between the monstrous work and himself. When he has satisfied himself, in general and in detail, that it was made by such a person as himself, so armed and so motivated, and to ends to which he himself in given circumstances should also have worked, the problem is then solved ; his thought lives along the whole line of temples and sphinxes and catacombs, passes through them all like a creative soul, with satisfaction, and they live again to the mind, or are *now.*

A gothic cathedral affirms that is was done by us, and not done by us. Surely it was by man, but we find it not in our man. But we apply ourselves to the history of its production. We put ourselves into the place and historical state of the builder. We remember the forest-dwellers, the first temples, the adherence to the first type, and the decoration of it as the wealth of the nation increased ; the value which is given to wood by carving led to the carving over the whole mountain of a stone cathedral. When we have gone through this process, and thereto the Catholic Church, its cross, its music, its processions, its Saints' days and image-worship, we have, as it were, been the man that made the minster ; we have seen how it could and must be. We have the sufficient reason.

The difference between men is in their principle of association. Some men classify objects by colour and size and other accidents of appearance ; others by intrinsic likeness, or by the relation of cause and effect. The progress of the intellect consists in the clearer vision of causes, which over-looks surface-differences. To the poet, to the philosopher, to the saint, all things are friendly and sacred, all events profitable, all days holy, all men divine. For the eye is fastened on the life, and slights the circumstance. Every chemical substance, every plant, every animal in its growth, teaches the unity of cause, the variety of appearance.

Why, being as we are surrounded by this all-creating nature, soft and fluid as cloud or the air, should we be such hard pedants, and magnify a few forms ? Why should we make account of time, or of magnitude, or of form ? The soul knows them not, and genius, obeying its law, knows how to play with them as a young child plays with greybeards and in churches. Genius studies the casual thought, and far back in the womb of things sees the rays parting from one orb, that diverge ere they fall by infinite diameters. Genius watches the monad through all his masks as he performs the metempsychosis of nature. Genius detects through the fly, through the caterpillar, through the grub, through the egg, the constant fixed species ; through many species the genus ; through all genera the steadfast type ; through all the kingdoms of organised life the eternal unity. Nature is a mutable cloud, which is always and never the same. She casts the same thought into troops of forms, as a poet makes twenty fables with one moral. Beautifully shines a spirit through the bruteness and toughness of matter. Alone omnipotent, it converts all things to its own end. The adamant streams into softest but precise form before it, but, whilst I look at it, its outline and texture are changed altogether. Nothing is so fleeting as form. Yet never does it quite deny itself. In man we still trace the rudiments or hints of all that we esteem badges of servitude in the lower races, yet in him they enhance his nobleness and grace ; as in Io, in Æschylus, transformed to a cow, offends the imagination, but how changed when as Isis in Egypt she meets Jove, a beautiful woman, with nothing of the metamorphosis left but the lunar horns as the splendid ornament of her brows !

The identity of history is equally intrinsic, the diversity equally obvious. There is at the surface infinite variety of things ; at the centre there is simplicity and unity of cause. How many are the acts of one man in which we recognise the same character ! See the variety of our sources of information in respect to the Greek genius. Thus at first we have the *civil history* of that people, Herodotus, Thucydides, Xenophon, Plutarch have given it—a very sufficient account of what manner of persons they were, and what they did. Then we have the same soul expressed for us again in their *literature* ; in poems, drama, and philosophy : a very complete form. Then we have it once more in their *architecture,*—the purest sensuous beauty,— the perfect medium never overstepping the limit of charming propriety and grace. Then we have it once more in *sculpture,*—" the tongue on the balance of expression," those forms in every action, at every age of life, ranging through all the scale of condition, from god to beast, and never transgressing the ideal serenity, but in convulsive exertion the liege of order and of law. Thus, of the genius of one remarkable people, we have found a fourfold representation,—the most various expression of one moral thing : and to the senses what more unlike than an ode of Pindar, a marble Centaur, the Peristyle of the Pantheon, and the last actions of Phocion ? Yet do these varied external expressions proceed from one national mind.

Every one must have observed faces and forms which, without any resembling feature, make a like impression on the beholder. A particular picture or copy of verses, if it do not awaken the same train of images, will yet superinduce the same sentiment as some wild mountain walk, although the resemblance is nowise obvious to the senses, but is occult and out of reach of the understanding. Nature is an endless combination and repetition of a very few laws. She hums the old well-known air through innumerable variations.

Nature is full of a sublime family-likeness throughout her works. She delights in startling us with resemblances in the most unexpected quarters. I have seen the head of an old sachem of the forest, which at once reminded the eye of a bald mountain summit, and the furrows of the brow suggested the strata of the rock. There are men whose manners have the same essential splendour as the simple and awful sculpture on the friezes of the Parthenon, and the remains of the earliest Greek art. And there are compositions of the same strain to be found in the books of all ages. What is Guido's Rospigliosi Aurora but a morning thought, as the horses in it are only a morning cloud. If any one will but take pains to observe the variety of actions to which he is equally inclined in certain modes of mind, and those to which he is averse, he will see how deep is the chain of affinity.

A painter told me that nobody could draw a tree without in some sort becoming a tree ; or draw a child by studying the outlines of its form merely,—but, by watching for a time his motions and plays, the painter enters his nature, and can then draw him at will in every attitude. So Roos " entered into the inmost nature of a sheep." I knew a draughtsman employed in a public survey, who found that he could not sketch the rocks until their geological structure was first explained to him.

What is to be inferred from these facts but this ; that in a certain state of thought is the common origin of very diverse works ? It is the spirit and not the fact that is identical. By descending far down into the depths of the soul, and not primarily by a painful acquisition of many manual skills, the artist attains the power of awakening other souls to a given activity.

It has been said that " common souls pay with what they do ; nobler souls with that which they are." And why ? Because a soul, living from a great depth of being, awakens in us by its actions and words, by its very looks and manners, the same power and beauty that a gallery of sculpture, or of pictures, are wont to animate.

Civil history, natural history, the history of art, and the history of literature,—all must be explained from individual history, or must remain words. There is nothing but is related to us, nothing that does not interest us—kingdom, college, tree, horse, or iron shoe, the roots of all things are in man. It is in the soul that the architecture exists. Santa Croce and the Dome of St. Peter's are lame copies after a divine model. Strasburg Cathedral is a material counterpart of the soul of Erin of Steinbach. The true poem is the poet's mind ; the true ship is the ship-builder. In the man, could we lay him open, we should see the sufficient reason for the last flourish and tendril of his work, as every spine and tint in the sea-shell pre-exist in the secreting organs of the fish. The whole of heraldry and chivalry is in courtesy. A man of fine manners shall pronounce your name with all the ornament that titles of nobility could ever add.

The trivial experience of every day is always verifying some old prediction to us, and converting into things for us also the words and signs which we had heard and seen without heed. Let me add a few examples, such as fall within the scope of every man's observation, of trivial facts which go to illustrate great and conspicuous facts.

A lady, with whom I was riding in the forest, said to me, that the woods always seems to her *to wait*, as if the genii who inhabit them suspended their deeds until the wayfarer has passed onward. This is precisely the thought which poetry has celebrated in the dance of the fairies, which breaks off on the approach of human feet. The man who has seen the rising moon break out of the clouds at midnight, has been present like an archangel at the creation of light and of the world. I remember that being abroad one summer day, my companion pointed out to me a broad cloud, which might extend a quarter of a mile parallel to the horizon, quite accurately in the form of a cherub as painted over churches,—a round block in the centre, which it was easy to animate with eyes and mouth, supported on either side by wide-stretched symmetrical wings. What appears once in the atmosphere may appear often, and it as undoubtedly the archetype of that familiar ornament. I have seen in the sky a chain of summer lighting which at once revealed to me that the Greeks drew from nature when they painted the thunderbolt in the hand of Jove. I have seen a snow-drift along the sides of the stone all which obviously gave the idea of the common architectural scroll to abut a tower.

By simply throwing ourselves into new circumstances we do continually invent anew the orders and ornaments of architecture, as we see how each people merely decorated its primitive abodes. The Doric temple still presents the semblance of the wooden cabin in which the Dorian dwelt. The Chinese pagoda is plainly a Tartar tent. The Indian and Egyptian temples still betray the mounds and subterranean houses of their forefathers. " The custom of making houses and tombs in the living rock, " (says Heeren, in his Researches on the Ethiopians), " determined very naturally the principal character of the Nubian Egyptian architecture to the colossal form which it assumed. In these caverns already prepared by nature, the eye was accustomed to dwell on huge shapes and masses, so that when art came to the assistance of nature, it could not move on a small scale without degrading itself. What would statues of the usual size, or neat porches and wings have been, associated with those gigantic halls before which only Colossi could sit as watchmen, or lean on the pillars of the interior ? "

The Gothic church plainly originated in a rude adaptation of the forest trees with all their boughs to a festal or solemn arcade, as the bands about the cleft pillars still indicate the green withes that tied them. No one can walk in a road cut through pine woods, without being struck by the architectural appearances of the groves, especially in winter, when the bareness of all other trees shows the low arch of the Saxons. In the woods in a winter afternoon one will see as readily the origin of the stained glass window with which the Gothic cathedrals are adorned, in the colours of the western sky seen through the bare and crossing branches of the forest. Nor can any lover of nature enter the old piles of Oxford and the English cathedrals without feeling that the forest over-powered the mind of the builder, and this his chisel, his saw, and plane still reproduced its ferns, its spikes of flowers, its locust, its pine, its oak, its fir, its spruce.

The Gothic cathedral is a blossoming in stone subdued by the insatiable demand of harmony in man. The mountain of granite blooms into an eternal flow with the lightness and delicate finish as well as the aerial proportions and perspective of vegetable beauty.

In like manner all public faces are to be individualised, all private facts are to be generalised. Then at once History becomes fluid and true, and Biography deep and sublime. As the Persian imitated in the slender shafts and capitals of his architecture the stem and flower of the lotus and palm, so the Persian court in its magnificent era never gave over the Nomadism of its barbarous tribes, but travelled from Ecbatana, where the spring was spent, to Susa in summer, and to Babylon for the winter.

In the early history of Asia and Africa, Nomadism and Agriculture are the two antagonistic facts. The geography of Asia and Africa necessitated a nomadic life. But the nomads were the terror of all those whom the soil or the advantages of a market had induced to build towns. Agriculture therefore was a religious injunction because of the perils of the state from nomadism. And in these late and civil countries of England and America, the contest of these propensities still fights out the old battle in each individual. We are all rovers and all fixtures by turns, and pretty rapid turns. The nomads of Africa are constrained to wander by the attacks of the gad-fly, which drives the cattle mad, and so compels the tribe to emigrate in the rainy season and drive off the cattle to the higher sandy regions. The nomads of Asia follow the pasturage from month to month. In America and Europe the nomadism is of trade and curiosity. A progress certainly from the gad-fly of Astraboras to the Anglo and Italomania of Boston Bay. The difference between men in this respect is the fault of rapid domestication, the power to find his chair and bed everywhere, which one man has, and another has not. Some men have so much of the Indian left, have constitutionally such habits of accommodation, that at sea, or in the forest, or in the snow, they sleep as warm, and dine with as good appetite, and associate as happily, as in their own house. And to push this old fact still one degree nearer, we may find it a representative of a permanent fact in human nature. The intellectual nomadism is the faculty of objectiveness, or of eyes which everywhere feed themselves. Who hath such eyes, everywhere falls into easy relations with his fellow-men. Every man, every thing is a prize, a study, a property to him, and this love soothes his brow, joins him to men, and makes him beautiful and beloved in their sight. His house is a waggon ; he roams through all latitudes as easily as a Calmuc.

Every thing the individual see without him, corresponds to his states of mind, and every thing is in turn intelligible to him, as his onward thinking leads him into the truth to which that fact or series belongs.

The primeval world, the Fore-World, as the Germans say,—I can dive to it myself as well as grope for it with researching fingers in catacombs, libraries, and the broken reliefs and torsos of ruined villas.

What is the foundation of that interest all men feel in Greek history, letters, art, and poetry, in all its periods, from the heroic or Homeric age, down to the domestic life of the Athenians and the Spartans, four or five centuries later ? This period draws us because we are Greeks. The Grecian state is the era of the bodily nature, the perfection of the senses,—of the spiritual nature unfolded in strict unity with the body. In it existed those human forms which supplied the sculptor with his models of Hercules, Phœbus, and Jove ; not like the forms abounding in the streets of modern cities, wherein the face is a confused blur of features, but composed of incorrupt, sharply defined and symmetrical features, whose eye-sockets are so formed that it would be impossible for such eyes to squint, and take furtive glances on this side and on that, but they must turn the whole head.

The manners of that period are plain and fierce. The reverence exhibited is for personal qualities, courage, address, self-command, justice, strength, swiftness, a loud voice, a broad chest. Luxury is not known, nor elegance. A sparse population and want make every man his own valet, cook, butcher, and solider ; and the habit of supplying his own needs educates the body to wonderful performances. Such are the Agamemnon and Diomed of Homer, and not far different is the picture Xenophon gives of himself and his compatriots in the Retreat of the Ten Thousand. " After the army had crossed the river Teleboas in Armenia, there fell much snow, and the troops lay miserably on the ground, covered with it. But Xenophon arose naked, and taking an axe, began to split wood ; whereupon others arose and did the like." Throughout his army seemed to be a boundless liberty of speech. They quarrel for plunder, they wrangle with the generals on each new order, and Xenophon is as sharp-tongued as any, and sharper-tongued than most, and so gives as good as he gets. Who does not see that this is a gang of great boys, with such a code of honour and such lax discipline as great boys have ?

The costly charm of the ancient tragedy, and indeed of all the old literature, is, that the persons speak simply—speak as persons who have great good sense without knowing it, before yet the reflective habit has become the predominant habit of the mind. Our admiration of the antique is not admiration of the old, but of the natural. The Greeks are not reflective but perfect in their senses, perfect in their health, with the finest physical organisation in the world. Adults acted with the simplicity and grace of boys. They made vases, tragedies, and statues such as healthy senses should—that is, in good taste.

Such things have continued to be made in all ages, and are now, wherever a healthy physique exists ; but, as a class, from their superior organisation, they have surpassed all. They combine the energy of manhood with the engaging unconsciousness of childhood. Our reverence for them is our reverence for childhood. Nobody can reflect upon an unconscious act with regret or contempt. Bard or hero cannot look down upon the word or gesture of a child. It is as great as they. The attraction of these manners is, that they belong to man, and are know to every man in virtue of his being once a child ; beside that always there are individuals who retain these characteristics. A person of childlike genius and inborn energy is still a Greek, and revives our love of the muse of Hellas. A great boy, a great girl, with good sense, is a Greek. Beautiful is the love of nature in the Philoctetes. But in reading those fine apostrophes to sleep, to the stars, rocks, mountains, and waves, I feel time passing away as an ebbing sea. I feel the eternity of man, the identity of his thought. The Greek had, it seems, the same fellow beings as I. The sun and moon, water and fire, met his heart precisely as they meet mine. Then the vaunted distinction between Greek and English, between Classic and Romantic schools, seems superficial and pedantic. When a thought of Plato becomes a thought to me,—when a truth that fired the soul of Pindar fires mine, time is no more. When I feel that we two meet in a perception, that our two souls are tinged with the same hue, and do, as it were, run into one, why should I measure degrees of latitude, why should I count Egyptian years ?

The student interprets the age of chivalry by his own age of chivalry, and the days of maritime adventure and circumnavigation by quite parallel miniature experiences of his own. To the sacred history of the world he has the same key. When the voice of a prophet out of the age of antiquity merely echoes to him a sentiment of his own infancy, prayer of his own youth, he then pierces to the truth though all the confusion of tradition and the caricature of institutions.

Rare, extravagant spirits come by us at intervals, who disclose to us new facts in nature. I see that men of God have always, from time to time, walked among men, and made their commission felt in the heart and soul of the commonest hearer. Hence, evidently, the tripod, the priest, the priestess inspired by the divine afflatus.

Jesus astonishes and overpowers sensual people. They cannot unite him to history, or reconcile him with themselves. As they come to revere their intuitions and aspire to live holily, their own piety explains every fact, every word.

How easily these old worships of Moses, or Zoroaster, of Menu, of Socrates, domesticate themselves in the mind ! I cannot find any antiquity in them. They are mine as much as theirs.

Then I have seen the first monks and anchorets without crossing seas or centuries. More than once some individual has appeared to me with such negligence of labour and such commanding contemplation, a haughty beneficiary, begging in the name of God, as made good to the nineteenth century Simeon the Stylite, the Thebais, and the first Capuchins.

The priestcraft of the East and West, of the Magian, Brahmin, Druid, and Inca, is expounded in the individual's private life. The cramping influence of a hard formalist on a young child in reprising his spirits and courage, paralysing the understanding, and that without producing indignation, but only fear and obedience, and even much sympathy with tyranny,—is a familiar fact explained to the child when he becomes a man, only by seeing that the oppressor of his youth is himself a child tyrannised over by those names and words and forms, of whose influence he was merely the organ to the youth. The fact teaches him how Belus was worshipped, and how the pyramids were built, better than the discovery by Champollion of the names of all the workmen and the cost of every tile. He finds Assyria and the Mounds of Cholula at his door, and himself has laid the courses.

Again, in that protest which each considerate person makes against the superstition of his times, he reacts step for step the part of old reformers, and is the search after again what mortal vigour is needed to supply the girdle of a superstition. A great licentiousness treads on the heels of a reformation. How many times in the history of the world has the Luther of the day had to lament the decay of piety in his own household ! " Doctor, " said his wife to Martin Luther one day, " how is it that whilst subject to papacy we prayed so often and with such fervour, while now we pray with the utmost coldness and very seldom ? "

The advancing man discovers how deep a property he hath in all literature,—in all fable as well as in all history. He finds that the poet was no odd fellow who described strange and impossible situations, but that universal man wrote by his pen a confession true for one and true for all. His own secret biography he finds in lines wonderfully intelligible to him, yet dotted down before he was born. One after another he comes up in his private adventures with every fable of Æsop, of Homer, of Hafiz, of Ariosto, of Chaucer, of Scott, and verifies them with his own head and hands.

The beautiful fables of the Greeks, being proper creations of the Imagination and not of the Fancy, are universal verities. What a range of meanings and what perpetual pertinence has the story of Prometheus ! Besides its primary value as the first chapter of the history of Europe (the mythology thinly veiling authentic facts, the invention of the mechanic arts, and the migration of the colonies), it gives the history of religion with some closeness to the faith of later ages. Prometheus is the Jesus between the unjust " justice " of the Eternal Father, and the race of mortals ; and readily suffers all things on their account. But where it departs from the Calvinistic Christianity, and exhibits him as the defier of Jove, it represents a state of mind which readily appears wherever the doctrine of Theism is taught in a crude, objective form, and which seems the self-defence of man against the untruth, namely, a discontent with the believed fact

that a God exists, and a feeling that the obligation of reverence is
onerous. It would steal, if it could, the fire of the Creator, and live
apart from him, and independent of him. The Prometheus Vinctus is
the romance of scepticism. Not less true to all time are all the details
of that stately apologue. Apollo kept the flocks of Admetus, said the
poets. Every man is a divinity in disguise, a god playing the fool. It
seems as if heaven had sent its insane angels into our world as to an
asylum, and here they will break out into their native music and utter
at intervals the words they have heard in heaven ; then the mad fit
returns, and they mope and wallow like dogs. When the gods come
among them, they are not known. Jesus was not ; Socrates and
Shakespeare were not. Antæus was suffocated by the gripe of
Hercules, but every time he touched his mother earth, his strength was
renewed. Man is the broken giant, and in all his weakness, both his
body and mind are invigorated by habits of conversation with nature.
The power of music, the power of poetry to unfix, and, as it were, clap
wings to all solid nature, interprets the riddle of Orpheus, which was to
his childhood an idle tale. The philosophical perception of identity
through endless mutations of form makes him know the Proteus. What
else am I who laughed or wept yesterday, who slept last night like a
corpse, and this morning stood and ran ? And what see I on any side
but the transmigrations of Proteus ? I can symbolise my thought by
using the name of any creature, of any fact, because every creature is
man agent or patient. Tantalus is but a name for you and me.
Tantalus means the impossibility of drinking the waters of thought
which are always gleaming and waving within sight of the soul. The
transmigration of souls : that too is no fable. I would it were ; but
men and women are only half human. Every animal of the barn-yard,
the field and the forest, of the earth and of the waters that are under the
earth, has contrived to get a footing, and to leave the print of its
features and form in some one or other of these upright, heaven-facing
speakers. Ah, brother, hold fast to the man and awe the beast ; stop
the ebb of thy soul—ebbing downward into the forms into whose
habits thou hast now for many years slid. As near and proper to us is
also the old fable of the Sphinx, who was said to sit in the roadside and

put riddles to every passenger. If the man could not answer, she swallowed him alive. If he could solve the riddle, the Sphinx was slain. What is our life but an endless flight of winged facts or events ? In splendid variety these changes come, all putting questions to the human spirit. Those men who cannot answer by a superior wisdom these facts or questions of time, serve them. Facts encumber them, tyrannise over them, and make the men of routine the men of *sense,* in whom a literal obedience to facts has extinguished every spark of that light by which man is truly man. But if a man is true to his better instincts or sentiments, and refuses the dominion of facts, as one that comes of a higher race, remains fast by the soul and sees the principle, then the facts fall aptly and supple into their places ; they know their master, and the meanest of them glorifies him.

See in Goethe's Helena the same desire that every world should be a thing. These figures, he would say, these Chirons, Griffins, Phorkyas, Helen, and Leda, are somewhat, and do exert a specific influence on the mind. So far then are they eternal entities, as real to-day as in the first Olympiad. Much revolving them, he writes out freely his humour, and gives them body to his own imagination. And although that poem be as vague and fantastic as a dream, yet it is much more attractive than the more regular dramatic pieces of the same author, for the reason that it operates a wonderful relief to the mind from the routine of customary images,—awakens the reader's invention and fancy by the wild freedom of the design, and by the unceasing succession of brisk shocks of surprise.

The universal nature, too strong for the petty nature of the bard, sits on his neck and writes through his hand ; so that when he seems to vent a mere caprice and wild romance, the issue is an exact allegory. Hence Plato said that " poets utter great and wise things which they do not themselves understand." All the fictions of the Middle Age explain themselves as a masked or frolic expression of that which, in grave earnest, the mind of that period toiled to achieve. Magic, and all that is ascribed to it, is manifestly a deep presentiment of the powers of science. The shoes of swiftness, the sword of sharpness, the power of subduing the elements, of using the secret virtues of minerals, of understanding the voices of birds, are the obscure efforts of the mind in a right direction. The preternatural prowess of the hero, the gift of perpetual youth, and the like, are alike the endeavour of the human spirit " to bend the shows of things to the desires of the mind."

In Perceforest and Amadis de Gaul, a garland and a rose bloom on the head of her who is faithful, and fade on the brow of the inconstant. In the story of the Boy and the Mantle, even a mature reader may be surprised with a glow of virtuous pleasure at the triumph of the gentle Genelas ; and, indeed, all the postulates of elfin annals, that the Fairies do not like to be named ; that their gifts are capricious and not to be trusted ; that who seeks a treasure must not speak ; and the like, I find true in Concord, however they might be in Cornwall or Bretagne.

Is it otherwise in the newest romance ? I read the Bride of Lammermoor. Sir William Ashton is a mask for a vulgar temptation, Ravenswood Castle, a fine name for proud poverty, and the foreign mission of state only a Bunyan disguise for honest industry. We may all shoot a wild bull that would toss the good and beautiful, by fighting down the unjust and sensual. Lucy Ashton is another name for fidelity, which is always beautiful and always liable to calamity in this world.

But along with the civil and metaphysical history of man, another history goes daily forward—that of the external world,—in which he is not less strictly implicated. He is the compend of time : he is also the correlative of nature. The power of man consists in the multitude of his affinities, in the fact that his life is intertwined with the whole chain of organic and inorganic being. In the age of the Cæsars, out from the Forum at Rome proceeded the great highways north, south, east, and west, to the centre of every province of the empire, making each market-town of Persia, Spain, and Britain, pervious to the soldiers of the capital : so out of the human heart go, as it were, highways to the heart of every object in nature, to reduce it under the dominion of man.   A man is a bundle of relations, a knot of roots, whose flower and fruitage is the world.   All his faculties refer to natures out of him.   All his faculties predict the world he is to inhabit, as the fins of the fish foreshow that water exists, or the wings of an eagle in the egg presuppose a medium like air.   Insulate, and you destroy him.   He cannot live without a world.   Put Napoleon in an island-prison, let his faculties find no men to act on, no Alps to climb, no stake to play for, and he would beat the air and appear stupid. Transport him to large countries, dense population, complex interests, and antagonist power, and you shall see that the man Napoleon, bounded, that is, by such a profile and outline, is not the virtual Napoleon.   This is but Talbot's shadow ;

> " His substance is not here :
> For what you see is but the smallest part,
> And least proportion of humanity ;
>
> But were the whole frame here,
> It is of such a spacious, lofty pitch,
> Your roof were not sufficient to contain it."
>
> *Henry VI*

Columbus needs a planet to shape his course upon.   Newton and Laplace needs myriads of ages and thick-strewn celestial areas.   One may say a gravitating solar system is already prophesied in the nature of Newton's mind.   Not less does the brain of Davy and Gay-Lussac from childhood, exploring always the affinities and repulsion's of particles, anticipate the laws of organisation.   Does not the eye of the human embryo predict the light ?   the ear of Handel predict the witchcraft of harmonic sound ?   Do not the constructive fingers of

Watt, Fulton, Whittemore, Arkwright predict the fusible, hard, and temperable texture of metals, the properties of stone, water, and wood ?   the lovely attributes of the maiden child predict the refinements and decorations of civil society ?   Here also we are reminded of the action of man on man.   A mind might ponder its thought for ages, and not gain so much self-knowledge as the passion of love shall teach it in a day.   Who knows himself before he has been thrilled with indignation at an outrage, or has heard an eloquent tongue, or has shared the throb of thousands in a national exultation or alarm ?   No man can antedate his experience, or guess what faculty or feeling a new object shall unlock, any more than he can draw to-day the face of a person whom he shall see to-morrow for the first time.

I will not now go behind the general statement to explore the reason of this correspondency.   Let it suffice that in the light of these two facts, namely, that the mind is One, and that nature is its correlative, history is to be read and written.

Thus in all ways does the the soul concentrate and reproduce its treasures for each pupil, for each new-born man.   He too shall pass through the whole cycle of experience.   He shall collect into a focus the rays of nature.   History no longer shall be a dull book.   It shall walk incarnate in every just and wise man.   You shall not tell me by languages and titles a catalogue of the volumes you have read.   You shall make me feel what periods you have lived.   A man shall be the Temple of Fame.   He shall walk, as the poets have described that goddess, in a robe painted all over with wonderful events and experiences ;—his own form and features by their exalted intelligence shall be that variegated vest.   I shall find in him the Foreword ; in his childhood the Age of Gold ; the Apples of Knowledge ; the Argonautic Expedition ; the calling of Abraham ; the building of the Temple ; the Advent of Reformation ; the discovery of new lands, the opening of new sciences, and new regions in man.   He shall be the priest of Pan, and bring with him into humble cottages the blessing of the morning stars and all the recorded benefits of heaven and earth.

Is there somewhat overweening in this claim ?   Then I reject all I have written ; for what is the use of pretending to know what we know not ?   But it is the fault of our rhetoric that we cannot strongly state one fact without seeming to belie some other.   I hold our actual knowledge very cheap.   Hear the rats in the wall, see the lizard on the fence, the fungus under foot, the lichen on the log.   What do I know sympathetically, morally, of either of these worlds of life ?   As long as the Caucasian man—perhaps longer—these creatures have kept their counsel beside him, and there is no record of any word or sign that has passed from one to the other.   Nay, what does history yet record of the metaphysical annals of man ?   What light does it shed on those mysteries which we hide under the names Death and Immortality ?   Yet every history should be written in a wisdom which divined the range of our affinities, and looked at facts as symbols.   I am ashamed to see what a shallow village-tale our so-called History is.   How many times must we say Rome, and Paris, and Constantinople.   What does Rome know of rat and lizard ?   What are Olympiads and Consulates to these neighbouring systems of being ?   Nay, what food or experience or succour have they for the Esquimaux seal-hunter, Kanàka in his canoe, for the fisherman, the stevedore, the porter ?

Broader and deeper we must write our annals—from an ethical reformation, from an influx of the ever-new, ever-sanative conscience —if we would truelier express our central and wide-related nature, instead of this old chronology of selfishness and pride to which we have too long lent our eyes.   Already that day exists for us, shines in on us at unawares ; but the path of science and of letters is not the way into nature, but from it rather.   The idiot, the Indian, the child, and the unschooled farmer's boy, come much nearer to these,—understand them better than the dissector or the antiquary.

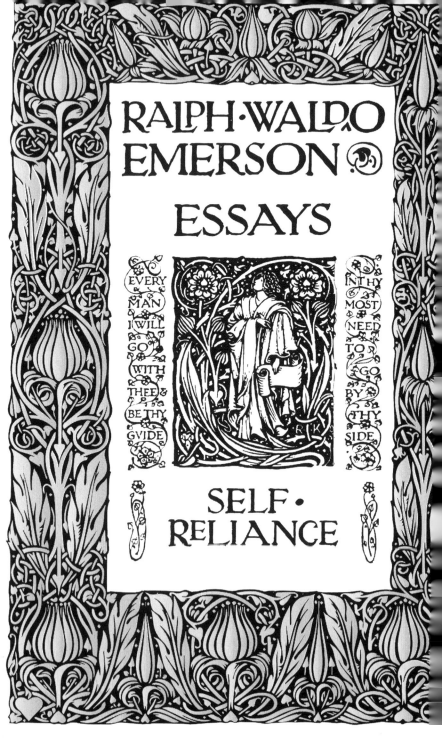

RALPH·WALDO
EMERSON

ESSAYS

EVERY MAN I WILL GO WITH THEE & BE THY GVIDE

IN THY MOST NEED TO GO BY THY SIDE

SELF·
RELIANCE

SELF-RELIANCE

Ne te quæsiveris extra.

"Man is his own star ; and the soul that can

Render an honest and a perfect man,

commands all light, all influence, all fate

Nothing to him falls early, or too late.

Our acts our angels are, or good, or ill,

our fatal shadows that walk by us still."

Epilogue to Beaumont and Fletcher's Honest Man's Fortune.

Edited by A.D Hendry
Cover Art by A.D Hendry

Cast the Bantling on the rocks,

Suckle him with the she-wolf's teat :

Wintered with the hawk and fox,

Power and speed be hands and feet.

I read the other day some verses written by an eminent painter which were original and not conventional.   Always a soul hears an admonition in such lines, let the subject be what it may.   The sentiment they instil is of more value than any thought they may contain.   To believe your own thought, to believe that what is true for you in your private heart, is true for all men,—that is genius.   Speak your latent conviction, and it shall be the universal sense ; for always the inmost becomes the outmost,—and our first thought is rendered back to us by the trumpets of the Last Judgement.   Familiar as the voice of mind is to each, the highest merit we ascribe to Moses, Plato, and Milton, is that they set at naught books and traditions, and spoke not what men but what they thought.   A man should learn to detect and watch for that gleam of light which flashes across his mind from within, more than the lustre of the firmament of bards and sages.   Yet he dismisses without notice his thought, because it is his.   In every work of genius, we recognise our own rejected thoughts : they come back to us with a certain alienated majesty.   Great works of art have no more affecting lesson for us than this.   They teach us to abide by our spontaneous impression with good-humoured inflexibility then most when the whole cry of voices is on the other side.   Else, tomorrow a stranger will say with masterly good sense precisely what we have thought and felt all the time, and we shall be forced to take with shame our own opinion from another.

There is a time in every man's education when he arrives at the conviction that envy is ignorance ; that imitation is suicide ; that he must take himself for better, or for worse, as his portion ; that though the wide universe is full of good, no kernel of nourishing corn can come to him but through his toil bestowed on that plot of ground which is given to him to till. The power which resides in him is new in nature, and none but he knows that which he can do, nor does he know until he has tried. Not for nothing one face, one character, one fact makes impression on him, and another none. It is not without pre-established harmony, this sculpture in the memory. The eye was placed where one ray should fall, that it might testify of that particular ray. Bravely let him speak the utmost syllable of his confession. We but half express ourselves, and are ashamed of the divine idea which each of us represents. It may be safely trusted as proportionate and of good issues, so it may be faithfully imparted, but God will not have his work made manifest by cowards. It needs a divine man to exhibit anything divine. A man is relieved and gay when he has put his heart into his work and done his best ; but what he has said or done otherwise, shall give him no peace. It is a deliverance which does not deliver. In the attempt his genius deserts him ; no muse befriends ; no invention, no hope.

Trust thyself : every heart vibrates to that iron string. Accept the place the divine Providence has found for you ; the society of your contemporaries, the connection of events. Great men have always done so, and confided themselves childlike to the genius of their age, betraying their perception that the eternal was stirring at their heart, working through their hands, predominating in all their being. And we are now men, and must accept in the highest mind the same transcendent destiny ; and not pinched in a corner, not cowards fleeing before a revolution, but redeemers and benefactors, pious aspirants to be noble clay plastic under the Almighty effort, let us advance and advance on Chaos and the Dark.

What pretty oracles nature yields us on this text in the face and behaviour of children, babes and even brutes ! That divided and rebel mind, that distrust of a sentiment because our arithmetic has computed the strength and means opposed to our purpose, these have not. Their mind being whole, their eye is as yet unconquered ; and when we look in their faces, we are disconcerted. Infancy conforms to nobody : all conform to it, so that one babe commonly makes four or five out of the adults who prattle and play with it. So God has armed youth and puberty and manhood no less with its own piquancy and charm, and made it enviable and gracious, and its claims not to be put by, if it will stand by itself. Do not think the youth has no force because he cannot speak to you and me. Hark ! in the next room, who spoke so clear and emphatic ? Good Heaven ! it is he ! it is that very lump of bashfulness and phlegm which for weeks has done nothing but eat when you were by, that now rolls out these words like bell-strokes. It seems he knows how to speak to his contemporaries. Bashful or bold, then, he will know how to make us seniors very unnecessary.

The nonchalance of boys who are sure of a dinner, and would disdain as much as a lord to do or say aught to conciliate one, is the healthy attitude of human nature. How is a boy the master of society ! Independent, irresponsible, looking out from his corner on such people and facts as pass by, he tries and sentences them on their merits, in the swift summary way of boys, as good, bad, interesting, silly, eloquent, troublesome. He cumbers himself never about consequences, about interests ; he gives an independent, genuine verdict. You must court him ; he does not court you. But the man is, as it were, clapped into jail by his consciousness. As soon as he has once acted or spoken with éclat, he is a committed person, watched by the sympathy or the hatred of hundreds, whose affections must now enter into his account. There is no Lethe for this. Ah, that he could pass again, into his neutral, godlike independence ! Who can thus lose all pledge, and having observed, observe again from the same unaffected, unbiased, unbribable, unaffrighted innocence, must always be formidable, must always engage the poet's and the man's regards. Of such immortal youth the force would be felt. He would utter opinions on all passing affairs, which being seen to not be private, but necessary, would sink like darts into the ear of men, and put them in fear.

These are the voices which we hear in solitude, but they grow faint and inaudible as we enter into the world.   Society everywhere is in conspiracy against the manhood of every one of its members.   Society is a joint-stock company, in which the members agree, for the better securing of his bread to each shareholder, to surrender the liberty and culture of the eater.   The virtue in most request is conformity.   Self-reliance is its aversion.   It loves no realities and creators, but names and customs.

Whoso would be a man must be a nonconformist.   He who would gather immortal palms must not be hindered by the name of goodness, but must explore if it be goodness.   Nothing is at last sacred but the integrity of our own mind.   Absolve you to yourself, and you shall have the suffrage of the world.   I remember an answer which, when quite young, I was prompted to make to a valued advisor who was wont to importune me with the dear old doctrines of the church.   On my saying, what have I to do with the sacredness of traditions, if I live wholly from within ? my friend suggested, —" But these impulses may be from below, not from above."   I replied, "They do not seem to be to be such, ; but if i am the devil's child, I will live then from the devil."   No law can be sacred to me but that of my nature.   Good and bad are but names, very readily transferable to that or this ; the only right way is what is after my constitution, the only wrong what is against it.   A man is to carry himself in the presence of all opposition as if every thing were titular and ephemeral but he.   I am ashamed to think how we easily we capitulate to badges and names, to large societies and dead institutions.   Every decent and well-spoken individual affects and sways me more than is right.   I ought to go upright and vital, and speak the rude truth in all ways.   If malice and vanity wear the cloak of philanthropy, will that pass ?   If an angry bigot assumes this bountiful cause of Abolition, and comes to me with his last news of Barbados, why should I not say to him, " Go, love thy infant ; love thy woodchopper : be good-natured and modest ; have that grace ; and never varnish your hard, uncharitable ambition with this incredible tenderness for black folk a thousand miles off.   Thy love afar is spite at home." Rough and graceless would be such greeting, but truth is handsomer than the affectation of love. Your goodness must have some edge to it —else it is none. The doctrine of hatred must be preached, as the counteraction of the doctrine of love when that pules and whines. I shun father and mother and wife and brother, when my genius calls me. I would write on the lintels of the door-post, Whim. I hope it is some-what better than whim at last, but we cannot spend the day in explanation. Expect me not to shew cause why I seek or why I exclude company. Then, again, do not tell me, as a good man did today, of my obligation to put all poor men in good situations. Are they my poor ? I tell thee, thou foolish philanthropist, that I grudge the dollar, the dime, the cent, I give to such men as do not belong to me, and to whom I do not belong. There is a class of persons to whom by all spiritual affinity I am bought and sold ; for them I will go to prison, if need be ; but your miscellaneous popular charities ; the education at college of fools ; the building of meeting houses to the vain end to which many now stand ; alms to sots ; and the thousandfold Relief Societies ;—though I confess with shame I sometimes succumb and give the dollar, it is a wicked dollar which by and by I shall have the manhood to withhold.

Virtues are, in the popular estimate, rather the exception than the rule. There is the man and his virtues. Men do what is called a good action, as some piece of courage or charity, much as they would pay a fine in expiation of daily non-appearance on parade. Their works are done as an apology or extenuation of their living in the world,—as invalids and the insane pay a high board. Their virtues are penances. I do not wish to expiate, but to live. My life is not an apology, but a life. It is for itself, and not for spectacle. I much prefer that it should be of a lower strain, so it be gentle and equal, that it should be glittering and unsteady. I wish it to be sound and sweet, and not to need diet and bleeding. My life should be unique ; it should be an alms, a battle, a conquest, a medicine. I ask primary evidence that you are a man, and refuse this appeal from the man to his actions. I know for myself it makes no difference whether I do or forbear those actions which are reckoned excellent. I cannot consent to pay for a privilege when I have intrinsic right. Few and mean as my gifts may be, I actually am, and do not need for my own assurance or the assurance of my fellows any secondary testimony.

What I must do, is all that concerns me ; not what the people think. This rule, equally arduous in actual and in intellectual life, may serve for the whole distinction between greatness and meanness. It is the harder, because you will always find those who think they know what is your duty better than you know it. It is easy in the world to live after the world's opinion ; it is easy in solitude to live after our own ; but the great man is he who in the midst of the crowd keeps with perfect sweetness the independence of solitude.

The objection to conforming to usages that have become dead to you, is, that it scatters your force. It loses your time, and blurs the impression of your character. If you maintain a dead church, contribute to a dead Bible-Society, vote with a great party either for the government or against it, spread your table like base house-keepers,— under all these screens, I have difficulty to detect the precise man you are. And, of course, so much force is withdrawn from your proper life. But do your thing, and I shall know you. Do your work, and you shall reinforce yourself. A man must consider what a blind-man's-bluff is this game of conformity. If I know your sect, I anticipate your argument. I hear a preacher announce for his text and topic the expediency of one of the institutions of the church. Do I not know beforehand that not possibly can he say a new and spontaneous word ? Do I not know that with all the ostentation of examining the grounds of the institution, he will do no such thing ? Do I not know that he is pledged to himself not to look but at one side ; the permitted side, not as a man, but as a parish minister ? He is a retained attorney, and these airs of the bench are the emptiest affectation. Well, most men have bound their eyes with one or another handkerchief, and attached themselves to some of these communities of opinion. This conformity makes them not false in a few particulars, authors of a few lies, but false in all particulars. Their every truth is not quite true. Their two is not the real two, their four not the real four : so that every word they say chagrins us, and we know not where to begin to set them right. Meantime nature is not slow to equip us in the prison-uniform of the party to which we adhere. We come to wear one cut of face and figure, and acquire by degrees the gentlest asinine expression. There is a mortifying experience in particular, which does not fail to wreak itself also in the general history ; I mean, " the foolish face of praise," the forced smile which we put on in company where we do not feel at ease in answer to conversation which does not interest us. The muscles, not spontaneously moved, but moved by a low usurping wilfulness, grow tight about the outline of the face, and make the most disagreeable sensation,—a sensation of rebuke and warning which no brave young man will suffer twice.

For nonconformity the world whips you with its displeasure. And therefore a man must know how to estimate a sour face. The bystanders look askance on him in the public street or in the friend's parlour. If this aversion had its origin in contempt and resistance like his own, he might well go home with a sad countenance ; but the sour faces of the multitude, like their sweet faces, have no deep cause,— disguise no god, but are put on and off as the wind blows and a newspaper directs. Yet is the discontent of the multitude more formidable than that of the senate and the college. It is easy enough for a firm man who knows the world to brook the rage of the cultivated classes. Their rage is decorous and prudent ; for they are timid, as being very vulnerable themselves. But when to their feminine rage the indignation of the people is added, when the ignorant and the poor are aroused, when the un-intelligent brute force that lies at the bottom of society is made to growl and mow, it needs the habit of magnanimity and religion to treat it godlike as a trifle of no concernment.

The other terror that scares us from self-trust is our consistency ; a reverence for our past act or word, because the eyes of others have no other data for computing our orbit than our past acts, and we are loath to disappoint them.

But why should you keep you head over your shoulder ? Why drag about this monstrous corpse of your memory, lest you contradict somewhat you have stated in this or that public space ? Suppose you should contradict yourself ; what then ? It seems to be a rule of wisdom never to rely on your memory alone, scarcely even in acts of pure memory, but bring the past for judgement into the thousand-eyed present, and live ever in a new day. Trust your emotion. In your metaphysics you have denied personality to the Deity : yet when the devout motions of the soul come, yield to them heart and life, though they should clothe God with shape and colour. Leave your theory, as Joseph his coat in the hands or the harlot, and flee.

A foolish consistency is the hobgoblin of little minds, adored by little statesmen and philosophers and divines. With consistency a great soul has simply nothing to do. He may as well concern himself with his shadow on the wall. Out upon your guarded lips ! Sew them up with packthread, do. Else, if you would be a man, speak what you think today in words as hard as cannon-balls, and tomorrow speak what tomorrow thinks in hard words again, though it contradict everything you said today. Ah, then exclaim the aged ladies, you shall be sure to be misunderstood. Misunderstood ! It is a right fool's word. Is it so bad then, to be misunderstood ? Pythagoras was misunderstood, and Socrates, and Jesus, and Luther, and Copernicus, and Galileo, and Newton, and every pure and wise spirit that ever took flesh. To be great is to be misunderstood.

I suppose no man can violate his nature. All the sallies of his will are rounded in by the laws of his being, as the inequalities of Andes and Himalaya are insignificant in the curve of the sphere. Nor does it matter how you gauge and try him. A character is like an acrostic or Alexandrian stanza ;—read it forward, backward, or across, it still spells the same thing. In this pleasing contrite wood-life which God allows me, let me record day by day my honest thought, without prospect or retrospect, and I cannot doubt it will be found symmetrical, though I mean it not, and see it not. My book should smell of pines and resound with the hum of insects. The swallow over my window should interweave that thread of straw he carries in his bill into my web also. We pass from what we are. Character teaches above our wills. Men imagine they communicate their virtue or vice only by overt actions, and do not see that virtue or vice emit a breath every moment.

Fear never but you shall be consistent in whatever variety of actions, so they be each honest and natural in their hour. For of one will the actions will be harmonious, however unlike they seem. These varieties are lost sight of when seen at a little distance, at a little height of thought. One tendency unites them all. The voyage of the best ship is a zig-zag line of a hundred tacks. This is only microscopic criticism. See the line from a sufficient distance, and it straightens itself to the average tendency. Your genuine action will explain itself, and explain your other genuine actions. Your conformity explains nothing. Act singly, and what you have already done singly will justify you now. Greatness always appeals to the future. If I can be great enough now to do right and scorn eyes, I must have done so much right before so as to defend me now. Be it how it will, do right now. Always scorn appearances and you always may. The force of character is cumulative. All the forgone days of virtue work their health into this. What makes the majesty of the heroes of the senate and the field, which so fills the imagination ? The consciousness of a train of great days and victories behind. There they all stand, and shed a united light on the advancing actor. He is attended as by an escort of angels visible to every man's eye. That is is which throws thunder into Chatham's voice, and dignity into Washington's port, and America into Adam's eye. Honour is venerable to us, because it is no ephemeris. It is always ancient virtue. We worship it today, because it is not of today. We love it and pay it homage, because it is not a trap for our love and homage, but is self-dependent, self-derived, and therefore of an old immaculate pedigree, even if shown in a young person.

I hope in these days we have heard the last of conformity and consistency. Let the words be gazetted and ridiculous henceforward. Instead of the gong for dinner, let us hear a whistle from the Spartan fife. Let us bow and apologise never more. A great man is coming to eat at my house. I do not wish to please him : I wish that he should wish to please me. I will stand here for humanity ; and though I would make it kind, I would make it true. Let us affront and reprimand the smooth mediocrity and squalid contentment of the times, and hurl in the face of custom, and trade, and office, the fact which is the upshot of all history, that there is a great responsible Thinker and Actor moving wherever moves a man ; that a true man belongs to no other time or place, but is the centre of things. Where he is, there is nature. He measures you, and all men, and all events. You are constrained to accept his standard. Ordinarily everyone in society reminds us of somewhat else or of some other person. Character, reality, reminds you of nothing else. It takes place of the whole creation. The man must be so much that he must make all circumstances indifferent,—put all means into the shade. This all great men are and do. Every true man is a cause, a country, and an age ; requires infinite spaces and numbers and time fully to accomplish his thought ;—and posterity seem to follow his steps as a procession.

A man Caesar is born, and for ages after we have a Roman Empire. Christ is born, and millions of minds so grow and cleave to his genius, that he is confounded with virtue and the possible of man. An institution is the lengthened shadow of one man, ; as the reformation of Luther ; Quakerism, of Fox ; Methodism, of Wesley ; Abolition, of Clarkson. Scipio, Milton called 'the height of Rome" ; and all history resolves itself very easily into the biography of a few stout and earnest persons.

Let a man, then, know his worth, and keep things under his feet. Let him not peep or steal, or skulk up and down with the air of a charity-boy, a bastard, or an interloper, in the world which exists for him. But the man in the street, finding no worth in himself which corresponds to the force which built a tower or sculptured a marble god, feels poor when he looks on these. To him, a palace, a statue, or a costly book have an alien and forbidding air, much like a gay equipage, and seem to say that, " Who are you, Sir ? " Yet they are all his, suitors for his notice, petitioners to his faculties that they will come out and take possession. The Picture waits for my verdict : it is not to command me, but I am to settle its claims to praise. That popular fable of the sot who was picked up dead drunk in the street, carried to the duke's house, washed and dressed and laid in the duke's bed, and, on his waking, treated with all obsequious ceremony like the duke, and assured that he had been insane,—owes popularity to the fact, that is symbolises so well that state of man, who is in the world a sort of sot, but now and then wakes up, exercises his reason, and finds himself a true prince.

Our reading is mendicant and sycophantic. In history, our imagination makes fools of us, plays us false. Kingdom and lordship, power and estate, are a gaudier vocabulary than private John and Edward in a small house and common day's work : but the things of life are the same to both ; the sum-total of both is the same. Why all this deference to Alfred, and Scanderbeg, and Gustavus ? Suppose they were virtuous : did they wear out virtue ? As great a stake depends on your private act today, as followed their public and renowned steps. When private men shall act with vast views, the lustre will be transformed from the acts of kings to those of gentlemen.

The world has indeed been instructed by its kings, who have so magnetised the eyes of nations. It has been taught by this colossal symbol the mutual reverence that is due from man to man. The joyful loyalty with which men have everywhere suffered the king, the noble, or the great proprietor to walk among them by a law of his own ; make his own scale of men and things, and reverse theirs ; pay for benefits not with money, but with honour, and represent the Law in his person,

— was the hieroglyphic by which they obscurely signified their consciousness of their own right and comeliness, the right of every man.

The magnetism which all original action exerts is explained when we inquire the reason of self-trust.   Who is the Trustee ?   What is the aboriginal Self on which a universal reliance may be grounded ?   What is the nature and power of that science-baffling star, without parallax, without calculable elements, which shoots a ray of beauty even into trivial and impure actions, if the least mark of independence appear ?   The inquiry leads us to that source, at once the essence of genius, the essence of virtue, and the essence of life, which we call spontaneity or instinct.   We denote this primary wisdom as Intuition, whilst all later teachings are tuitions.   In that deep force, the last fact, behind which analysis cannot go, all things find their common origin. For the sense of being, which in calm hours rises, we know not how, in the soul, is not diverse from things, from space, from light, from time, from man, but one with them, and proceeds obviously from the same source whence their life and being also proceeds.   We first share the life by which things exist, and afterwards see them as appearances in nature, and forget that we have shared their cause.   Here is the fountain of action and the fountain of thought.   Here are the lungs of inspiration which giveth man wisdom, of that inspiration which cannot be denied without impiety and atheism.   We lie in the lap of immense intelligence, which makes us organs of its activity and receivers of its truth.   When we discern justice, when we discern truth, we do nothing of ourselves but allow a passage to its beams.   If we ask whence this comes, if we seek to pry into the soul of that causes, all metaphysic, all philosophy is at fault.   Its presence or absence is all we can affirm. Every man discerns between the voluntary acts of his mind, and his involuntary perceptions.   And to his involuntary perceptions he knows a perfect respect is due.   He may err in the impression of them, but he knows that these things are so, like day and night, not to be disputed. All my wilful actions and acquisitions are but roving ;—the most trivial reverie, the faintest emotion are domestic and divine.

Thoughtless people contradict as readily the statement of perceptions as of opinions, or rather much more readily ; for they do not distinguish between perception and notion.   They fancy that I choose to see this or that thing.   But perception is not whimsical, but fatal.   If I see a trait, my children will see it after me, and in course of time all mankind,—although it may chance that no one has seen it before me. For my perception of it is as much a fact as the sun.

The relations of the soul to the divine spirit are so pure that it is profane to seek to interpose helps.   It must be that when God speaks, he should communicate not one thing, but all things ; should fill the world with his voice ; should scatter forth light, nature, time, souls, from the centre of the present thought ; and new date and new create the whole.   Whenever a mind is simple, and receives a divine wisdom, then old things pass away, —means, teachers, texts, temples fall ; it lives now, and absorbs past and future into the present hour.All things are made sacred by relation to it,—one thing as much as another. All things are dissolved to their centres by their cause, and in the universal miracle petty and particular miracles disappear.   This is and must be.   If, therefore, a man claims to know and speak of God, and carries you back to the phraseology of some old mouldered nation in another country, in another world, believe him not.   Is the acorn better than the oak, which is it's fullness and completion ?   Is the parent better than the child into whom he has cast his ripened being ? Whence then this worship of the past ?   The centuries are conspirators against the sanity and majesty of the soul.   Time and space are but physiological colours which the eye makes, but the soul is light ; where it is, is day ; where it was, is night ; and history is an impertinence and an injury, if it be anything more than a cheerful apologue or parable of my being and becoming.

Man is timid and apologetic.   He is no longer upright.   He dares not say " I think," " I am," but quotes some saint or sage.   He is ashamed before the blade of grass or the blowing rose.   These roses under my window make no reference to former roses or to better ones ;

they are what they are ; they exist with God today. There is no time to them. There is simply the rose ; it is perfect in every moment of its existence. Before a leaf-bud has burst, its whole life acts ; in the full-blown flower there is no more ; in the leafless root there is no less. Its nature is satisfied and it satisfies nature, in all moments alike. There is no time to it. But man postpones or remembers ; he does not live in the present, but with reverted eyes laments the past, or, to foresee the future. He cannot be happy and strong until he too lives with nature in the present, above time. This should be plain enough, yet see what strong intellects dare not yet hear God himself, unless he speak the phraseology of I know not what David, or Jeremiah, or Paul. We shall not always set so great a price on a few texts, on a few lives. We are like children who repeat by rote the sentences of grandames and tutors, and, as they grow older, of the men of talents and character they chance to see,—painfully recollecting the exact words they spoke ; afterwards, when they come into the point of view which those had who uttered these sayings, they understand them, and are willing to let the words go ; for, at any time, they can use words as good, when occasion comes. So was it with us ; so will it be, if we proceed. If we live truly, we shall see truly. It is as easy for the strong man to be strong, as it is for the weak to be weak. When we have new perception, we shall gladly disburden the memory of its hoarded treasures as old rubbish. When a man lives with God, his voice shall be as sweet as the murmur of the brook and the rustle of the corn.

And now at last the highest truth on this subject remains unsaid, probably cannot be said ; for all that we say is the far-off remembering of the intuition. That thought, by what I can now nearest approach to say it, is this. When good is near you, when you have life in yourself, —it is not by any known or appointed way ; you shall not discern the footprints of any other ; you shall not se the face of man ; you shall not hear any name ;—the way, the thought, the good, shall be wholly strange and new. It shall exclude all other being. You take the way from man, not to man. All persons that ever existed are its fugitive ministers. There shall be no fear in it. Fear and hope are alike beneath it. It asks nothing. There is somewhat low even in hope. We are then in vision. There is nothing that can be called gratitude nor properly joy. The soul is raised over passion. It seethes identity and eternal causation. It is a perceiving that Truth and Right are. Hence it becomes a tranquility out of knowing that all things go well. Vast spaces of nature, the Atlantic Ocean, the South Sea ; vast intervals of time, years, centuries, are of no account. This which I think and feel, underlay that former state of life and circumstances, as it does underlie my present, and will always all circumstance, and what is called life, and what is called death.

Life only avails, not the having lived. Power ceases in the instant of repose ; it resides in the moment of transition from a past to a new state ; in the shooting of the gulf, in the darting to an aim. This one fact the world hates, that the soul becomes ; for that forever degrades the past ; turns all riches to poverty, all reputation to a shame ; confounds the saint with the rogue ; shoves Jesus and Judas equally aside. Why then do we prate of self-reliance ? Inasmuch as the soul is present, there will be power not confident but agent. To talk of reliance, is a poor external way of speaking. Speak rather of that which relies, because it works and is. Who has more soul that I master me, though he should not raise his finger. Round him I must revolve by the gravitation of spirits ; who has less, I rule like facility. We fancy it rhetoric when we speak of eminent virtue. We do not yet see that virtue is Height, and that a man or a company of men plastic and permeable to principles, by the law of nature must overpower and ride all cities, nations, kings, rich men, poets, who are not.

This is the ultimate fact which we so quickly reach on this as on every topic, the resolution of all into the ever-blessed ONE. Virtue is the governor, the creator, the reality. All things real are so by so much of virtue as they contain. Hardship, husbandry, hunting, whaling, war, eloquence, personal weight, are somewhat, and engage my respect as examples of the soul's presence and impure action. I see the same law working in nature for conservation and growth. The poise of a planet, the bended tree recovering itself from a strong wind, the vital resources of every vegetable and animal, are also demonstrations of the self-sufficing, and therefore self-relying soul. All history, from its highest to its trivial passages, is the various record of this power.

Thus all concentrates : let us not rove ; let us sit at home with the cause. Let us stun and abolish the intruding rabble of men and books and institutions by a simple declaration of the divine fact. Bid them take their shoes from off their feet, for God is here within. Let our simplicity judge them, and our docility to our own law demonstrate the poverty of nature and fortune beside our native riches.

But now we are a mob. Man does not stand in awe of man, nor is the soul admonished to stay at home, to put itself in communication with the internal ocean, but it goes abroad to beg a cup of water of the urns of men. We must go alone. Isolation must precede true society. I like the silent church before the service begins, better than any preaching. How far off, how cool, how chaste the persons look, begirt each one with a precinct or sanctuary ! So let us always sit. Why should we assume the faults of our friend, or wife, or father, or child, because they sit around our hearth, or are said to have the same blood ? All men have my blood, and I have all men's. Not for that will I adopt their petulance or folly, even to the extent of being ashamed of it. But your isolation not be mechanical, but spiritual, that is, must be elevation. At times the whole world seems to be in conspiracy to importune you with emphatic trifles. Friend, client, child, sickness, fear, want, charity, all knock out at once at thy closest-door and say, " Come out unto us."—Do not spill thy soul ; do not all descend ; keep thy state ; stay at home in thine own heaven ; come out for a moment into their facts, into their hubbub of conflicting appearances, but let in the light of thy law on their confusion. The power men possess to annoy me, I give them by a weak curiosity. No man can come near me but through my act. " What we love, that we have ; but by desire we bereave ourselves of the love."

If we cannot at once rise to the sanctities of obedience and faith, let us at least resist our temptations, let us enter into the state of war, and wake Thor and Wotan, courage and constancy, in our Saxon breasts. This is to be done in our smooth times by speaking the truth. Check this lying hospitality and lying affection. Live no longer to the expectation of these deceived and deceiving people with whom we converse. Say to them, O father, O mother, O wife, O brother, O friend, I have lived with you after appearances hitherto. Henceforward I am the truth's. Be it known unto you that henceforward I obey no law less than the eternal law. I will have no covenants but proximities. I shall endeavour to nourish my parents, to support my family, to be the chaste husband of one wife,—but these relations I must fill after a new and unprecedented way. I appeal from your customs. I must be myself. I cannot break myself any longer for you, or you. If you can love me for what I am, we shall be the happier. If you cannot, I will still seek to deserve that you should. I must be myself. I will not hide my tastes or aversions. I will so trust that what is deep is holy, that I will do strongly before the sun and moon whatever inly rejoices me, and the heart appoints. If you are noble, I will love you ; If you are not, I will not hurt you and myself by hypocritical attentions. If you are true, but not in the same truth with me, cleave to your companions ; I will seek my own. I do this not selfishly, but humbly and truly. It is alike your interest and mine and all men's, however long we have dwelt in lies, to live in truth. Does this sound harsh today ? You will soon love what is dictated by your nature as well as mine ; and if we follow the truth, it will bring us out safe at last.—But so you may give these friends pain. Yes, but I cannot sell my liberty and my power, to save their sensibility. Besides, all persons have their moments of reason, when they look out into the region of absolute truth ; then they will justify me and do the same thing.

The populace thinks that your rejection of popular standards is a rejection of all standard, and mere antinomianism ; and the bold sensualist will use the name of philosophy to gild his crimes. But the law of consciousness abides.   There are two confessionals, in one or the other of which we must be shriven.   You may fulfil your round of duties by clearing yourself in the direct, or in the reflex way. Consider whether you have satisfied your relations to father, mother, cousin, neighbour, town, cat, and dog ; whether any of these can upbraid you.   But I may also reject this reflex standard, and absolve me to myself.   I have my own stern claims and perfect circle.   It denies the name of duty to many offices that are called duties.   But if I can discharge its debts, it enables me to dispense with the popular code.   If anyone imagines that this law is lax, let him keep its commandment one day.

And truly it requires something godlike in him who has cast off the common motives of humanity, and has ventured to trust himself for a task-maker.   High be his heart, faithful his will, clear his sight, that he may in good earnest be doctrine, society, law to himself, that a simple purpose may be to him as strong as iron necessity is to others.

If any man consider the present aspects of what is called by distinction society, he will see the need of these ethics.   The sinew and heart of man seem to be drawn out, and we are becoming timorous desponding whimperers.   We are afraid of truth, afraid of fortune, afraid of death, and afraid of each other.   Our age yields no great and perfect persons.   We want men and women who shall renovate life and our social state, but we see that most natures are insolvent ; cannot satisfy their own wants, have an ambition out of all proportion to their practical force, and so do lean and beg day and night continually.   Our housekeeper is mendicant, our arts, our occupations, our marriages, our religion we have not chosen, but society has chosen for us.   We are parlour soldiers.   The rugged battle of fate, where strength is born, we shun.   If our young men miscarry in their first enterprises, they lose all heart.   If the young merchant fails, men say he is ruined.   If the finest genius studies at one of our colleges, and is not installed in an office within one year afterwards in the cities or suburbs of Boston or New York, it seems to his friends and to himself that he is right in being disheartened and in complaining the rest of his life. A sturdy lad from New Hampshire or Vermont, who in turn tries all the professions, who teams it, farms it, peddles, keeps a school, preaches, edits a newspaper, goes to Congress, buys a township, and so forth, in successive years, and always, like a cat, falls on his feet, is worth a hundred of these city dolls. He walks abreast with his days, and feels no shame in not " studying a profession," for he does not postpone his life, but lives already. He has not one chance, but a hundred chances. Let a stoic arise who shall reveal the resources of man, and tell me they are not leaning willows, but can and must detach themselves ; that with the exercise of self-trust, new powers shall appear ; that a man is the word made flesh, born to shed healing to the nations ; that he should be ashamed of our compassion ; and that the moment he acts from himself, tossing the laws, the books, idolatries, and customs out of the window, we pity him no more, but thank and revere him ;—and that teacher shall restore the life of man to splendour, and make his name dear to all history.

It is easy to see that a greater self-reliance,—a new respect for the divinity in man,—must work a revolution in all the offices and relations of men ; in their religion ; in their education ; in their pursuits ; their modes of living ; their association ; in their property ; in their speculative views.

1.   In what prayers do men allow themselves ! That which they call a holy office, is not so much as brave and manly. Prayer looks abroad, and asks for some foreign addition to come through some foreign virtue, and loses itself in endless mazes of natural and supernatural, and mediatorial and miraculous. Prayer that craves a particular commodity—any thing less than all good, is vicious. Prayer is the contemplation of the facts of life from the highest point of view. It is the soliloquy of a beholding and jubilant soul. It is the spirit of God pronouncing his works good. But prayer as a means to affect a private end, is theft and meanness. It supposes dualism and not unity in nature and consciousness. As soon as the man is at one

with God, he will not beg.   He will then see all prayer in action.   The prayer of the rower kneeling with the stroke of his oar, are true prayers heard throughout nature, through the cheap ends.   Caratach, in Fletcher's Bonduca, when admonished to inquire the mind of the god Andate, replies,

"His hidden meaning lies in our endeavours,

Our valours are our best gods."

Another sort of false prayers are our regrets.   Discontent is the want of self-reliance : it is the infirmity of will.   Regret calamities, if you can thereby help the sufferer ; if not, attend your own work, and already the evil begins to be repaired.   Our sympathy is just as base. We come to them who weep foolishly, and sit down and cry for company, instead of imparting to them truth and health in rough electric shocks, putting them once more in communication with the soul.   The secret of fortune is joy in our hands.   Welcome evermore to the gods and men is the self-helping man.   For him all doors are flung wide.   Him all tongues greet, all honours crown, all eyes follow with desire.   Our love goes out to him and embraces him, because he did not need it.   We solicitously and apologetically caress and celebrate him, because he held on his way and scorned our disapprobation.   The gods love him, because men hated him.   " To the preserving mortal," said Zoroaster, " the blessed Immortals are swift."

As a men's prayers are a disease of the will, so are their creeds a disease of the intellect.   They say with those foolish Israelites, " Let not God speak to us, lest we die.   Speak thou, speak any man with us, and we will obey."   Everywhere I am bereaved of meeting God in my brother, because he has shut his own temple doors, and recites fables merely of his brother's, or his brother's brother's God.   Every new mind is a new classification.   If it prove a mind of uncommon activity and power, a Locke, a Lavoisier, a Hutton, a Bentham, a Spurzheim, it imposes its classification on other men, and lo ! a new system.   In proportion always to the depth of the thought, and so to the number of objects it touches and brings within reach of the pupil, is his complacency. But chiefly is this apparent in creeds and churches, which are also classifications of some powerful mind acting on the great elemental thought of Duty, and man's relation to the Highest. Such is Calvanism, Quakerism, Swedenborgianism. The pupil takes the same delight in subordinating every thing to the new terminology, that a girl does who has just learned botany, in seeing a new earth and new seasons thereby. It will happen for a time, that the pupil will feel a real debt to the teacher,—will find his intellectual power has grown by the study of his writings. This will continue until he has exhausted his master's mind. But in all unbalanced minds the classification is idolised, passes for the end, and not for a speedily inexhaustible means, so that the walls of the system blend to their eye in the remote horizon with the walls of the universe ; the luminaries of heaven seem to them hung on the arch their master built. They cannot imagine how you aliens have any right to see,—how you can see ; " It must be somehow that you stole the light from us." They do not yet perceive, that light unsystematic, indomitable, will break into any cabin, even into theirs. Let them chirp awhile and call it their own. If they are honest and do well, presently their neat new pinfold will be too strait and low, will crack, will lean, will rot and vanish, and the immortal light, all young and joyful, million-orbed, million-coloured, will beam over the universe as on the first morning.

2.   It is for the want of self-culture that the idol of Travelling, the idol of Italy, of England, of Egypt, remains for all educated Americans. They who made England, Italy, or Greece venerable in the imagination did so not by rambling round the creation as a moth round a lamp, but by sticking fast where they were, like an axis of the earth. In manly hours we feel that duty is our place, and that merrymen of circumstance should follow as they may. The soul is no traveller : the wise man stays at home with the soul ; and when his necessities, his duties, or any occasion call him from his house, or into foreign lands, he it at home still, and is not gadding abroad by himself, and shall make men sensible by the expression of his countenance, that he goes

the missionary of wisdom and virtue, and visits cities and men like a
sovereign, and not like an interloper or a valet. I have no churlish
objection to the circumnavigation of the globe for the purposes of art,
of study, and benevolence, so that the man is first domesticated, or
does not go abroad with the hope of finding somewhat greater than he
knows. He who travels to be amused, or to get somewhat which he
does not carry, travels away from himself, and grows old even in youth
among young things. In Thebes, in Palmyra, his will and mind have
become old and dilapidated as they. He carries ruins to ruins.

Travelling is a fool's paradise. We owe to our first journeys the
discovery that place is nothing. At home I dream that at Naples, at
Rome, I can be intoxicated with beauty, and lose my sadness. I pack
my trunk, embrace my friends, embark on the sea, and at last wake up
in Naples, and there beside me is the stern Fact, the sad Self,
unrelenting, identical, that I fled from. I seek the Vatican, and the
palaces. I affect to be intoxicated with sights and suggestions, but I
am not intoxicated. My giant goes with me wherever I go.

3.   But the rage of travelling is itself only a symptom of a deeper
unsoundness, affecting the whole intellectual action. The intellect is
vagabond, and the universal system of education fosters restlessness.
Our minds travel when our bodies are forced to stay at home. We
imitate ; and what is imitation but the travelling of the mind ? Our
houses are built with foreign taste ; our shelves are garnished with
foreign ornaments ; our opinions, our tastes, our whole minds lean, and
follow the Past and the Distant, as the eyes of a maid follow her
mistress. The soul created the arts wherever they have flourished. It
was in his own mind that the artist sought his model. It was an
application of his own thought to the thing to be done and the
conditions to be observed. And why need we copy the Doric or the
Gothic model ? Beauty, convenience, grandeur of thought, and quaint
expression, are as near to us as to any ; and if the American artists will
study with hope and love the precise thing to be done by him,
considering the climate, the soil, the length of day, the wants of the

people, the habit and form of the government, he will create a house in which all these will find themselves fitted, and taste and sentiment will be satisfied also. Insist on yourself ; never imitate. Your own gift you can present every moment with the cumulative force of a whole life's cultivation ; but of the adopted talent of another you have only extemporaneous, half-possession. That which each can do best, none but his maker can teach him. No man yet knows what is, nor can, till that person has exhibited it. Where is the master who could have taught Shakespeare ? Where is the master who could have instructed Franklin, or Washington, or Bacon, or Newton ? Every great man is an unique. The Scipionism of Scipio is precisely that part he could not borrow. If any body will tell me whom the great man imitates in the original crisis when he performs a great act, I will tell him who else than himself can teach him. Shakespeare will never be made by the study of Shakespeare. Do that which is assigned thee, and thou canst not hope too much or dare too much. There is at this moment, there is for me an utterance bare and grand as that of the colossal chisel of Phidias, or trowel of the Egyptians, or the pen of Moses, or Dante, but different from all these. Not possibly will the soul all rich, all eloquent, with thousand-cloven tongue, deign to repeat itself ; but if I can hear what these patriarchs say, surely I can reply to them in the same pitch of voice : for the ear and the tongue are two organs of one nature. Dwell up there in the simple and noble regions of thy life, obey thy heart, and thou shalt reproduce the Foreword again.

4.   As our Religion, our Education, our Art look abroad, so does our spirit of society. All men plume themselves on the improvement of society, and no man improves.   Society never advances. It recedes as fast on one side as it gains on the other. Its progress is only apparent, like the workers of a treadmill. It undergoes continual changes : it is barbarous, it is civilised, it is christened, it is rich, it is scientific ; but this change is not amelioration. For every thing that is given, something is taken. Society acquires new arts, and loses old instincts. What a contrast between the well-clad, reading, writing, thinking American, with a watch, a pencil, and a new bill of exchange

in his pocket, and the naked New Zealander, whose poverty is a club, a spear, a mat, and an undivided twentieth of a shed to sleep under ! But compare the health of these two men, and you shall see that his aboriginal strength the white man has lost. If the traveller tell us truly, strike the savage with a broad axe, and in a day or two the flesh shall unite and heal as if you struck the blow into soft pitch, and the same blow shall send a white man to his grave.

The civilised man has built a coach, but has lost the use of his feet. He is supported on crutches, but loses so much support of muscle. He has got a fine Geneva watch, but he has lost the skill to tell the hour by the sun. A Greenwich nautical almanac he has, and so being sure of the information when he wants it, the man in the street does not know a star in the sky. The solstice he does not observe ; the equinox he knows as little ; and the whole bright calendar of a year is without a dial in his mind. His note-books impair his memory ; his libraries overload his wit ; the insurance office increases the number of accidents ; and it may be a question whether machinery does not encumber ; whether we have not lost by refinement some energy, by a Christianity entrenched in establishments and forms some vigour of wild virtue. For every stoic was a stoic ; but in Christendom where is the Christian ?

There is no more deviation in the moral standard than in the standard of height or bulk. No greater men are now than ever were. A singular equality may be observed between the great men of the first and of the last ages ; nor can all the science, art, religion and philosophy of the nineteenth century avail to educate greater men than Plutarch's heroes, three or four and twenty centuries ago. Not in time is the race progressive. Phocion, Socrates, Anaxagoras, Diogenes, are great men, but they leave no class. He who is really of their class will not be called by their name, but be wholly his own man, and in his turn the founder of a sect. The arts and inventions of each period are only its costume, and do not invigorate men. The harm of the improved machinery may compensate its good. Hudson and Behring accomplished so much in their fishing boats, as to astonish Parry and Franklin, whose equipment exhausted the resources of science and art. Galileo, with an opera-glass, discovered a more splendid series of facts than any one since. Columbus found the new world in an un-decked boat. It is curious to see the periodical disuse and perishing of means and machinery which were introduced with loud laudation a few years or centuries before. The great genius returns to essential man. We reckoned the improvements of the art of war among the triumphs of science, and yet Napoleon conquered Europe by the Bivouac, which consisted of falling back on naked valour, and dismembering it of all aids. The Emperor held it impossible to make a perfect army, says Las Casas " Without abolishing our arms, magazines, commissaries, and carriages ; until, in imitation of the Roman custom, the soldier should receive his supply of corn, grind it in the hand-mill and bake his bread himself. "

Society is a wave. The waves move onward, but the water of which it is composed does not. The same particle does not rise from the valley to the ridge. Its unity is only phenomenal. The persons who make up a nation today, next year die, and their experience with them

And so the reliance on Property, including the reliance on governments to protect it, is the want of self-reliance. Men have looked away from themselves at things so long, they they have come to esteem what they call the soul's progress, namely, the religious, learned, and civil institutions, as guards of property, and they depreciate assaults on these, because they feel them to be assaults on property. They measure their esteem of each other by what each has, and not by what each is. But a cultivated man becomes ashamed of his property, ashamed of what he has, out of a new respect for his being. Especially he hates what he has, if he see that it is accidental, —came to him by inheritance, or gift, or crime ; then he feels that it is not having ; it does not belong to him, has no root in him, and merely lies there, because no revolution or no robber takes it away. But that which a man is, does always by necessity acquire, and what the man acquires is permanent and living property, which does not wait for the beck of rulers, or mobs, or revolutions, of fire, or storm, or bankruptcies, but perpetually renews itself wherever the man is put. " Thy lot or portion of life," said the Caliph Ali, " is seeking after thee ; therefore be at rest from seeking after it."   Our dependence on foreign goods leads us to our slavish respect for numbers.   The political parties meet in numerous conventions ; the greater the concourse, and with each new uproar of announcement, The delegation from Essex !   The Democrats from New Hampshire !   The Whigs of Maine !   The young patriot feels himself stronger than before by a new thousand of eyes and arms.   In like manner the reformers summon conventions, and note and resolve in multitude.   But not so, O friends ! will the God deign to enter and inhabit you ; but by a method precisely the reverse.   It is only as a man puts off from himself all external support, and stands alone, that I see him to be strong and to prevail.   He is weaker by every recruit to his banner.   Is not a man better than a town ?   Ask nothing of men, and in the endless mutation, thou only firm column must appear the upholder of all that surrounds thee.   He who knows that power is in the soul, that he is weak only because he has looked for good out of him and elsewhere, and so perceiving, throws himself unhesitatingly on his thought, instantly rights himself, stands in the erect position, commands his limbs, works miracles ; just as a man who stands on his feet stronger is than a man who stands on his head.

So use all that is called Fortune.   Most men gamble with her, and gain all, and lose all, as her wheel rolls.   But do thou leave as unlawful these winnings, and deal with Cause and Effect, the chancellors of God.   In the Will work and acquire, and thou hast chained the wheel of Chance, and shall always drag her after thee.   A political victory, a rise of rents, the recovery of your sick, or the return of your absent friend, or some other quite external event, raises your spirits, and you think good days are preparing for you.   Do not believe it. It can never be so. Nothing can bring you peace but yourself. Nothing can bring you peace but the triumph of principles.

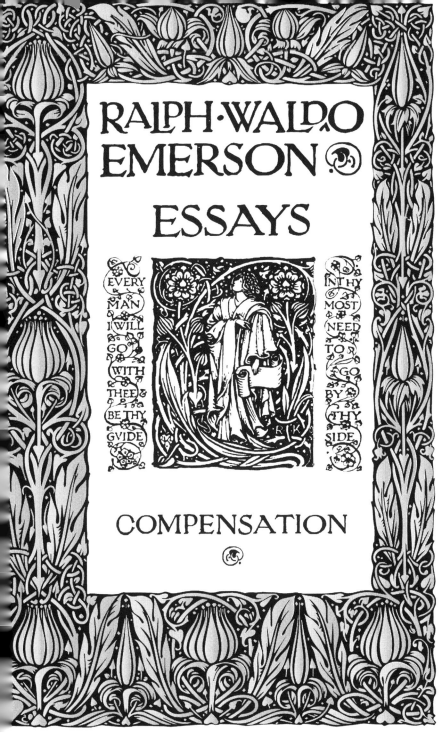

RALPH·WALDO EMERSON

ESSAYS

EVERY MAN I WILL GO WITH THEE & BE THY GVIDE

IN THY MOST NEED TO GO BY THY SIDE

COMPENSATION

COMPENSATION

Edited by A.D Hendry
Cover Art by A.D Hendry

Ever since I was a boy, I have wished to write a discourse on Compensation : for it seemed to me when very young, that, on this subject, Life was ahead of theology, and the people knew more than the preachers taught. The documents, too, from which the doctrine is to be drawn, charmed my fancy by their endless variety, and lay always before me, even in sleep ; for they are the tools in our hands, the bread in our basket, the transaction of the street, the farm, and the dwelling-house, the greetings, the relations, the debts and credits, the influence of character, the nature and endowment of all men. It seemed to me also that it might be shewn men a ray of divinity, the present action of the Soul of this world, clean from all vestige of tradition, and so the heart of man might be bathed by an inundation of eternal love, conversing with that which he knows was always and always must be, because it really is now. It appeared, moreover, that if this doctrine could be stated in terms with any resemblance to those bright intuitions in which this truth is sometimes revealed to us, it would be a star in many dark hours and crooked passages in our journey, that would not suffer us to lose our way.

I was lately confined in these desires by hearing a sermon at church. The preacher, a man esteemed for his orthodoxy, unfolded in the ordinary manner the doctrine of the Last Judgement. He assumed that judgement is not executed in this world ; that the wicked are successful ; that the good are miserable ; and then urged from reason and from Scripture a compensation to be made to both parties in the next life. No offence appeared to be taken by the congregation at this doctrine. As far as I could observe, when the meeting broke up, they separated without remark on the sermon.

Yet what was the impart of this teaching ? What did the preacher mean by saying that the good are miserable in the present life ? Was it that houses, and lands, offices, wine, horses, dress, luxury, are had by unprincipled men, whilst the saints are poor and despised ; and that a compensation is to be made to these last hereafter, by giving them the like gratifications another day,—bank-stock and doubloons, venison and champagne ? This must be the compensation intended ; for what else ? Is it that they are to have leave to pray and praise ? to love and serve men ? Why, that they can do now. The legitimate inference the disciple would draw, was : " We are to have *such* a good time as the sinners have now " ;—or, to push it to its extreme import : " You sin now ; we shall sin by and by : we would sin now, if we could ; not being successful, we expect our revenge to-morrow."

The fallacy lay in the immense concession that the bad are successful ; that justice is not done now. The blindness of the preacher consisted in referring to the base estimate of the market of what constitutes a manly success, instead of confronting and convicting the world from the truth ; announcing the Presence of the Soul, the omnipotence of the Will ; and so establishing the standard of good and ill, of success and falsehood, and summoning the dead to its present tribunal.

I find a similar base tone in the popular religious works of the day, and the same doctrines assumed by literary men when occasionally they treat the related topics. I think that our popular theology has gained in decorum, and not in principle, over the superstitions it has displaced. But men are better than this theology. Their daily life gives it the lie. Every ingenious and aspiring soul leaves the doctrine behind him in his own experience ; and all men feel sometimes the falsehood which they cannot demonstrate. For men are wiser than they know. That which they hear in schools and pulpits without afterthought, if said in conversation would probably be questioned in silence. If a man dogmatise in a mixed company on Providence and the divine laws, he is answered by a silence which conveys well enough to an observer the dissatisfaction of the hearer, but his incapacity to make his own statement.

I shall attempt in this and the following chapter to record some facts that indicate the path of the law of Compensation ; happy beyond my expectation, if I shall truly draw the smallest arc of this circle.

POLARITY, or action and reaction, we meet in every part of nature ; in darkness and light ; in heat and cold ; in the ebb and flow of waters ; in male and female ; in the inspiration and expiration of plants and animals ; in the systole and diastole of the heart ; in the undulations of fluid and of sound ; in the centrifugal and centripetal gravity ; in electricity, galvanism, and chemical affinity.   Superinduce magnetism at one end of a needle, the opposite magnetism takes place at the other end.   If the south attracts, the north repels.   To empty here, you must condense there.   An inevitable dualism bisects nature, so that each thing is a half, and suggests another thing to make it whole ; as spirit, matter ; man, woman ; subjective, objective ; in, out ; upper, under ; motion, rest ; yea, nay.

While the world is thus dual, so is every one of its parts.   The entire system of things gets represented in each particle.   There is somewhat that resembles the ebb and flow of the sea, day and night, man and woman, in a single needle of the pine, in a kernel of corn, in each individual of every animal tribe.   The reaction so grand in the elements is repeated within these small boundaries.   For example, in the animal kingdom, the physiologist has observed that no creatures are favourites, but a certain compensation balances every gift and every defect.   A surplusage given to one part is paid out of a reduction from another part of the same creature.   If the head and neck are enlarged, the trunk and extremities are cut short.

The theory of the mechanic forces is another example.   What we gain in power is lost in time ; and the converse.   The periodic or compensating errors of the planets is another instance.   The influences of climate and soil in political history are another.   The cold climate invigorates ; the barren soil does not breed fevers, crocodiles, tigers, or scorpions.

The same dualism underlies the nature and condition of man.   Every excess causes a defect ; every defect an excess.   Every sweet hath its sour ; every evil its good.   Every faculty which is a receiver of pleasure, has an equal penalty put on its abuse.   It is to answer for its

moderation with its life.   For every grain of wit there is a grain of
folly.   For every thing you have missed, you have gained something
else ; and for everything you gain, you lose something.   If riches
increase, they are increased that use them.   If the gatherer gathers too
much, nature takes out of the man what she puts into his chest ; swells
the estate, but kills the owner.   Nature hates monopolies and
exceptions.   The waves of the sea do not more speedily seek a level
from their loftiest tossing, than the varieties of condition tend to
equalise themselves.   There is always some levelling circumstance,
that puts down the overbearing, the strong, the rich, the fortunate,
substantially on the same ground with all others.   Is a man too strong
and fierce for society, and by temper and position a bad citizen,—a
morose ruffian with a dash of the pirate in him ;—nature sends him a
troop of pretty sons and daughters, who are getting along in the dame's
classes at the village-school, and love and fear for them smooths his
grim scowl to courtesy.   Thus she contrives to intenerate the granite
and felspar, takes the boar out and put the lamb in, and keeps her
balance true.

The farmer imagines power and place are fine things.   But the
President has payed dear for his White House.   It has commonly cost
him all his peace and the best of his manly attributes.   To preserve for
a short time so conspicuous an appearance before the world, he is
content to eat dust before the real masters, who stand erect behind the
throne.   Or, do men desire the more substantial and permanent
grandeur of genius ?   Neither has this an immunity.   He who by force
of will or of thought is great, and overlooks thousands, has the
responsibility of overlooking.   With every influx of light comes new
danger.   Has he light ? he must bear witness to the light, and always
outrun that sympathy which gives him such keen satisfaction, by his
fidelity to new revelations of the incessant soul.   He must hate father
and mother, wife and child.   Has he all that the world loves and
admires and covets ?   he must cast behind him their admiration, and
afflict them by faithfulness to his truth, and become a by-word and a
hissing.

This law writes the laws of cities and nations. It will not be baulked of its end in the smallest iota. It is in vain to build or plot or combine against it. Things refuse to be mismanaged long. *Res nolunt diu male administrari.* Though no checks to a new evil appear, the checks exist, and will appear. If the government is cruel, the governor's life is not safe. If you tax too high, the revenue will yield nothing. If you make the criminal code sanguinary, juries will not convict. Nothing arbitrary, nothing artificial can endure. The true life and satisfaction of man seem to elude the utmost rigours or felicities of condition, and to establish themselves with great indifferency under all varieties of circumstance. Under all governments the influence of character remains the same,—in Turkey and in New England about alike. Under the primeval despots of Egypt, history honestly confesses that man must have been as free as culture could make him.

These appearances indicate the fact that the universe is represented in every one of its particles. Every thing in nature contains all the powers of nature. Every thing is made of one hidden stuff ; as the naturalist sees one type under every metamorphosis, and regards a horse as a running man, a fish as a swimming man, a bird as a flying man, a tree as a rooted man. Each new form repeats not only the main character of the type, but part for part, all the details, all the aims, furtherances, hinderances, energies, and whole system of every other. Every occupation, trade, art, transaction, is a compend of the world, and a correlative of every other. Each one is an entire emblem of human life ; of its good and ill, its trials, its enemies, its course, and its end. And each one must somehow accommodate the whole man, and recite all his destiny.

The world globes itself in a drop of dew. The microscope cannot find the animalcule which is less perfect for being little. Eyes, ears, taste, smell, motion, resistance, appetite, and organs of reproduction that take hold on eternity,—all found room to consist in the small creature. So do we put our life into every act. The true doctrine of omnipresence is, that God reappears with all his parts in every moss and cobweb.   The value of the universe contrives to throw itself into every point.   If the good is there, so is the evil ; if the affinity, so the repulsion ; if the force, so the limitation.

Thus is the universe alive.   All things are moral.   That soul which within us is a sentiment, outside of us is a law.   We feel its inspirations ; out there in history we can see its fatal strength.   It is almighty.   All nature feels its grasp.   " It is in the world, and the world was made by it."   It is eternal, but it enacts itself in time and space.   Justice is not postponed.   A perfect equity adjusts itself in all parts of life.

Αεί γαρ εΰ πίπτουσιν οι Διός κύβοι.

The dice of God are always loaded.

The world looks like a multiplication-table or a mathematical equation, which, turn it how you will, balances itself.   Take what figure you will, its exact value, nor more nor less, still returns to you. Every secret is told, every crime is punished, every virtue rewarded, every wrong redressed, in silence and certainty.   What we call retribution, is the universal necessity by which the whole appears wherever a part appears.   If you see smoke, there must be a fire.   If you see a hand or a limb, you know that the trunk to which it belongs is there behind.

Every act rewards itself, or, in other words, integrates itself, in a twofold manner ; first, in the thing, or in real nature ; and secondly, in the circumstance, or in apparent nature.   Men call the circumstance the retribution.   The causal retribution is in the thing, and is seen by the soul.   The retribution in the circumstance is seen by the understanding ; it is inseparable from the thing, but is often spread over a long time, and so does not become distinct until after many years.   The specific stripes may follow later after the offence, but they follow because they accompany it.   Crime and punishment grow out of one stem.   Punishment is a fruit that unsuspected ripens within the flower of the pleasure which concealed it.   Cause and effect, means and ends, seed and fruit, cannot be severed ; for the effect already blooms in the cause, the end pre-exists in the means, the fruit in the seed.

Whilst the world will be whole, and refuses to be disparted, we seek to act partially, to sunder, to appropriate ; for example,—to gratify the senses, we sever the pleasure of the sense from the needs of the character.   The ingenuity of man has been dedicated always to the solution of one problem,—how to detach the sensual sweet, the sensual strong, the sensual bright, &c., from the moral sweet, the moral deep, the moral fair ; that is, again, to contrive to cut clean off this upper surface so thin as to leave it bottomless ; to get a *one end*, without an *other end.*   The soul says, The man and woman shall be one flesh and one soul ; the body would join the flesh only.   The soul says, Have dominion over all things to the ends of virtue ; the body would have the power over things to its own ends.

The soul strives amain to live and work through all signs.   It would be the only fact.   All things shall be added unto it,—power, pleasure, knowledge, beauty.   The particular man aims to be somebody ; to set up for himself ; to truck and higgle for a private good ; and, in particulars, to ride, that he may ride ; to dress, that he may be dressed ; to eat, that he may eat ; and to govern, that he may be seen. Men seek to be great ; they would have offices, wealth, power, and fame.   They think that to be great is to get only one side of nature— the sweet, without the other side—the bitter.

Steadily is this dividing and detaching counteracted.   Up to this day, it must be owned, no projector has had the smallest success.   The parted water reunites behind our hand.   Pleasure is taken out of pleasant things, profit out of profitable things, power out of strong things, the moment we seek to separate them from the whole.   We can no more halve things, and get the sensual good by itself, than we can get an inside that shall have no outside, or a light without a shadow. " Drive out nature with a fork, she comes running back."

Life invests itself with inevitable conditions, which the unwise seek to dodge, which one and another brags that he does not know ; brags that they do not touch him ;—but the brag is on his lips, the conditions are in his soul.   If he escapes them in one part, they attack him in another vital part.   If he has escaped them in form and in the appearance, it is that he has resisted his life and fled from himself ; and the retribution is so much death.   So signal is the failure of all attempts to make this separation of the good from the tax, that the experiment would not be tried,—since to try it is to be mad,—but for the circumstance, that when the disease begins in the will, or rebellion and separation, the intellect is at once infected, so that the man ceases to see God whole in each object, and not see the sensual hurt ; he sees the mermaid's head, but not the dragon's tail ; and thinks he can cut off that which he would have, from that which he would not have.
" How secret art thou who dwellest in the highest heavens in silence, O thou only great God, sprinkling with an unwearied Providence certain penal blindnesses upon such as have unbridled desires ! "[1]

The human soul is true to these facts in the painting of fables, of history, of law, of proverbs, of conversation.   It finds a tongue in literature unawares.   Thus the Greeks called Jupiter, Supreme Mind ; but having traditionally ascribed to him many base actions, they involuntarily made amends to Reason, by tying up the hands of so bad a god.   He is made as helpless as a king of England.   Prometheus knows one secret, which Jove must bargain for ; Minerva, another. He cannot get his own thunders ; Minerva keeps the key of them.

" Of all the gods I only know the keys

That ope the solid doors within whose vaults

His thunders sleep."

---

[1] St. Augustine : Confessions, book i.

A plain confession of the in-working of the All, and of its moral aim.   The Indian mythology ends in the same ethics ; and indeed it would seem impossible for any fable to be invented and get any currency which was not moral.   Aurora forgot to ask youth for her lover, and so though Tithonus is immortal, he is old.   Achilles is not quite invulnerable ; for Thetis held him by the heel when she dipped him in the Styx, and the sacred waters did not wash that part. Siegfried, in the Nibelungen, is not quite immortal, for a leaf fell on his back whilst he was bathing in the Dragon's blood, and that spot which it covered is mortal.   And so it always is.   There is a crack in everything God has made.   Always, it would seem, there is this vindictive circumstance stealing in at unawares, even into the the wild posey in which the human fancy attempted to make bold holyday, and to shake itself free of the old laws,—this backstroke, this kick of the gun, certifying that the law is fatal ; that in Nature nothing can be given, all things are sold.

This is the ancient doctrine of Nemesis, who keeps watch in the Universe, and lets no offence go unchastened.   The Furies, they said, are attendants on Justice, and if the sun in heaven should transgress his path, they would punish him.   The poets related that stone walls, and iron swords, and leathern thongs, had an occult sympathy with the wrongs of their owners ; that the belt which Ajax gave Hector dragged the Trojan hero over the field at the wheels of the car of Achilles ; and the sword which Hector gave Ajax was that on whose point Ajax fell. They recorded, that when the Thasians erected a statue to Theogenes, a victor in the games, one of his rivals went to it by night, and endeavoured to throw it down by repeated blows, until at last he removed it from its pedestal, and was crushed to death beneath its fall.

The voice of fable has in it somewhat divine.   It came from the thought above the will of the writer.   That is the best part of each writer which has nothing private in it.   That is the best part of each which he does not know, that which flowed out of his constitution, and not from his too active invention ; that which in the study of a single artist you might not easily find, but in the study of many you would abstract as the spirit of them all.   Phidias it is not, but the work of man in that early Hellenic world, that I would know.   The name and circumstance of Phidias, however convenient for history, embarrasses when we come to the highest criticism.   We are to see that which man was tending to in a given period, and was hindered, or, if you will, modified in doing, by the interfering volitions of Phidias, of Dante, of Shakespeare, the organ whereby man at the moment wrought.

Still more striking is the expression of this fact in the proverbs of all nations, which are always the literature of Reason, or the statements of an absolute truth without qualification.   Proverbs, like the sacred books of each nation, are the sanctuary of the Intuitions.   That which the droning world, chained to appearances, will not allow the realist to say in his own words, it will suffer him to say in proverbs without contradiction.   And this law of laws, which the pulpit, the senate, and the college deny, is hourly preached in all markets and all languages by flights of proverbs, whose teaching is as true and as omnipresent as that of birds and flies.

All things are double, one against another.—Tit for tat ; an eye for an eye ; a tooth for a tooth ; blood for blood ; measure for measure ; love for love.—Give, and it shall be given you.—He that watereth shall be watered himself.—What will you have ?   quoth God ; pay for it, and take it.—Nothing venture, nothing have.—Thou shalt be paid exactly for what thou hast done, no more, no less.—Who doth not work shall not eat.—Harm watch, harm catch.—Curses always recoil on the head of him who imprecates them.—If you put a chain around the neck of a slave, the other end fastens itself around your own.—Bad counsel confounds the adviser.—The devil is an ass.

It is thus written, because it is thus in life.   Our action is overmastered and characterised above our will by the law of nature. We aim at a petty end, quite aside from the public good, but our act arranges itself by irresistible magnetism in a line with the poles of the world.

A man cannot speak but he judges himself.   With his will, or against his will, he draws his portrait to the eye of his companions by every word.   Every opinion reacts on him who utters it.   It is a threadbare thrown at a mark, but the other end remains in the thrower's bag.   Or rather, it is a harpoon thrown at the whale, unwinding, as it flies, a coil of cord in the boat ; and if the harpoon is not good, or not well thrown, it will go nigh to cut the steersman in twain, or to sink the boat.

You cannot do wrong without suffering wrong.   " No man had ever a point of pride that was not injurious to him," said Burke.   The exclusive in fashionable life does not see that he excludes himself from enjoyment, in the attempt to appropriate it.   The exclusionist in religion does not see that he shuts the door of heaven on himself, in striving to shut out others.   Treat men as pawns and ninepins, and you shall suffer as well as they.   If you leave out their heart, you shall lose your own.   The senses would make things of all persons ; of women, of children, of the poor.   The vulgar proverb, " I will get it from his purse or get it from his skin," is sound philosophy.

All infractions of love and equity in our social relations are speedily punished.   They are punished by Fear.   Whilst I stand in simple relations to my fellow man, I have no displeasure in meeting him.   We meet as water meets water, or a current of air meets another, with perfect diffusion and interpenetration of nature.   But as soon as there is any departure from simplicity and attempt at halfness, or good for me that is not good for him, my neighbour feels the wrong ; he shrinks from me as far as I have shrunk from him ; his eyes no longer seek mine ; there is war between us ; there is hate in him, and fear in me.

All the old abuses in society, the great and universal, and the petty and particular, all unjust accumulations of property and power, are avenged in the same manner.   Fear is an instructor of great sagacity, and the herald of all revolutions.   One thing he always teaches, that there is rottenness where he appears.   He is a carrion crow ; and though you see not well what he hovers for, there is death somewhere. Our property is timid, our laws are timid, our cultivated classes are timid.   Fear for ages has boded and mowed and gibbered over government and property.   That obscene bird is not there for nothing. He indicates great wrongs, which must be revised.

Of the like nature is that expectation of change which instantly follows the suspension of our voluntary activity. The terror of cloudless moon, the emerald of Polycrates, the awe of prosperity, the instinct which leads every generous soul to impose on itself tasks of a noble asceticism and vicarious virtue, are the tremblings of the balance of justice through the heart and mind of man.

Experienced men of the world know very well that it is always best to pay scot and lot as they go along, and that a man often pays dear for a small frugality.   The borrower runs his own debt.   Has a man gained anything who has received a hundred favours and rendered none ?   Has he gained by borrowing, through indolence or cunning, his neighbours wares, or horses, or money ?   There arises on the deed the instant acknowledgement of benefit on the one part, and of debt on the other ; that is, of superiority and inferiority.   The transaction remains in the memory of himself and his neighbour ; and every new transaction alters, according to its nature, their relation to each other. He may soon come to see that he had better have broken his own bones that to have ridden in his neighbour's coach, and that " the highest price he can pay for a thing is to ask for it."

A wise man will extend this lesson to all parts of his life, and know that it is always the part of prudence to face every claimant, and pay every just demand on your time, your talents, or your heart.   Always pay ; for first or last, you must pay your entire debt.   Persons and events may stand for a time between you and justice, but it is only a postponement.   You must pay at last your own debt.   If you are wise, you will dread a prosperity which only loads you with more.   Benefit is the end of nature.   But for every benefit which you receive, a tax is levied.   He is great who confers the most benefits.   He is base,—and that is the one base thing in the universe,—to receive favours, and render none.   In the order of nature we cannot render benefits to those from whom we receive them, or only seldom.   But the benefit we receive must be rendered again, line for line, deed for deed, cent for cent, to somebody.   Beware of too much good staying in your hand. It will fast corrupt and worm worms.   Pay it away quickly in some sort.

Labour is watched over by the same pitiless laws.   Cheapest, say the prudent, is the dearest labour.   What we buy in a broom, a mat, a wagon, a knife, is some application of good sense to a common want. It is best to pay in your land a skilful gardener, or to buy good sense applied to gardening ; in your sailor, good sense applied to navigation ; in the house, good sense applied to cooking, sewing, and serving ; in your agent, good sense applied to accounts and affairs.   So do you multiply your presence, or spread yourself throughout your estate. But because of the dual constitution of all things, in labour as in life there can be no cheating.   The thief steals from himself.   The swindler swindles himself.   For the real price of labour is knowledge and virtue, whereof wealth and credit are signs.   These signs, like paper-money, may be counterfeited or stolen, but that which they represent, namely, knowledge and virtue, cannot be counterfeited or stolen.   These ends of labour cannot be answered but by real exertions of the mind, and in obedience to pure motives.   The benefit, cannot extort the knowledge of material and moral nature, which his honest care and pains yield to the operative.   The law of nature is, Do the thing, and you shall have the power : but they who do not the thing have not the power.

Human labour, through all its forms, from the sharpening of a stake to the construction of a city or an epic, is one immense illustration of the perfect compensation of the universe.   Every where and always this law is sublime.   The absolute balance of Give and Take, the doctrine that every thing has its price ; and if that price is not paid, not that thing, but something else, is obtained, and that it is impossible to get anything without its price,—this doctrine is not less sublime in the columns of a ledger than in the budget of states, the laws of light and darkness, in all the action and reaction of nature. I cannot doubt that the high laws which each man sees ever implicated in those processes with which he is conversant, the stern ethics which sparkle on his chisel-edge, which are measured out by his plumb and foot-rule, which stand as manifest in the footing of the shop-bill as in the history of a state,—do recommend to him his trade, and though seldom named, exalt his business to his imagination.

The league between virtue and nature engages all things to assume a hostile front to vice. The beautiful laws and substances of the world prosecute and whip the traitor. He finds that things are arranged for truth and benefit, but there is no den in the wide world to hide a rogue. There is no such thing as concealment. Commit a crime, and the earth is made of glass. Commit a crime, and it seems as if a coat of snow fell on the ground, such as reveals in the woods the track of every partridge and fox and squirrel and mole. You cannot recall the spoken word, you cannot wipe out the foot-track, you cannot draw up the ladder, so as to leave no inlet or clew. Always some damning circumstance transpires. The laws and substances of nature, water, snow, wind, gravitation, become penalties to the thief.

On the other hand, the law holds with equal sureness for all right action. Love, and you shall be loved. All love is mathematically just, as much as the two sides of an algebraic equation. The good man has absolute good, which like fire turns every thing to its own nature, so that you cannot do him any harm ; but as the royal armies sent against Napoleon, when he approached, cast down their colours, and from enemies became friends, so do disasters of all kinds, as sickness, offence, poverty, prove benefactors.

" Winds blow and waters roll

Strength to the brave, and power and deity,

Yet in themselves are nothing."

The good are befriended even by weakness and defect.   As no man had ever a point of pride that was not injurious to him, so no man ever had a defect that was not somewhere made useful to him.   The stag in the fable admired his horns and blamed his feet ; but when the hunter came, his feet saved him, and afterwards, caught in the thicket, his horns destroyed him.   Every man in his lifetime needs to thank his faults.   As no man thoroughly understands a truth until first he has contended against it, so no man has a thorough acquaintance with the hinderances or talents of men, until he has suffered from the one, and seen the triumph of the other over his own want of the same.   Has he a defect of temper that unfits him to live in society ?   Thereby he is driven to entertain himself alone, and acquire habits of self-help ; and thus, like the wounded oyster, he mends his shell with pearl.

Our strength grows out of our weakness.   Not until we are pricked and stung and sorely shot at, awakens the indignation which arms itself with secret forces.   A great man is always willing to be little.   Whilst he sits on the cushion of advantages, he goes to sleep.   When he is pushed, tormented, defeated, he has a chance to learn something ; he has been put on his wits, on his manhood ; he has gained facts ; learns his ignorance ; is cured of the insanity of conceit ; has got moderation and real skill.   The wise man always throws himself on the side of his assailants.   It is more his interest than it is there's to find his weak point.   The wound cicatrises and falls off from him, like a dead skin ; and when they would triumph, lo !   he has passed on invulnerable. Blame is safer than praise.   I hate to be defended in a newspaper.   As long as all that is said, is said against me, I feel a certain assurance of success.   But as soon as honied words of praise are spoken for me, I feel as one that lies unprotected before his enemies.   In general, every evil to which we do not succumb is a benefactor.   As the sandwich islander believes that the strength and colour of the enemy he kills passes into himself, so we gain the strength of the temptation we resist.

The same guards which protect us from disaster, defect, and enmity, defend us, if we will, from selfishness and fraud. Bolts and bars are not the best of our institutions, nor is shrewdness in trade a mark of wisdom. Men suffer all their life long under the foolish superstition that they can be cheated. But it is as impossible for a man to be cheated by any one but himself, as for a thing to be and not to be at the same time. There is a third silent party to all our bargains. The nature and soul of things takes on itself the guaranty of the fulfilment of every contract, so that the honest service cannot come to loss. If you serve an ungrateful master, serve him more. Put God in your debt. Every stroke shall be repaid. The longer the payment is withholden, the better for you ; for compound interest on compound interest is the rate and usage of this exchequer.

The history of persecution is a history of endeavours to cheat nature, to make water run up hill, to twist a rope of sand. It makes no difference whether the actors be many or one, a tyrant or a mob. A mob is a society of bodies voluntarily bereaving themselves of reason and traversing its work. The mob is a man voluntarily descending to the nature of the beast. Its fit hour of activity is night. Its actions are insane, like its whole constitution. It persecutes a principle ; it would whip a right ; it would tar-and-feather justice, by inflicting fire and outrage upon the houses and persons of those of who have these. It resembles the prank of boys who run with fire-engines to put out the ruddy aurora streaming to the stars. The inviolate spirit turns their spite against the wrong-doers. The martyr cannot be dishonoured. Every lash inflicted is a tongue of fame ; every prison a more illustrious abode ; every burned book or house enlightens the world ; every suppressed or expunged word reverberates through the earth from side to side. The minds of men are at last aroused ; reason looks out and justifies her own, and malice finds all her work vain. It is the whipper who is whipped, and the tyrant who is undone.

Thus do all things preach the indifferency of circumstances. The man is all. Every advantage has its tax. I learn to be content. But

the doctrine of compensation is not the doctrine of indifferency.   The
thoughtless say, on hearing these representations : What boots it to do
well ? there is one event to good and evil : if I gain any good, I must
pay for it ; if I lose any good, I gain some other ; all actions are
indifferent.

There is a deeper fact in the soul than compensation ; to wit, its
own nature.   The soul is not a compensation, but a life.   The soul *is*.
Under all this running sea of circumstance, whose waters ebb and flow
with perfect balance, lies the aboriginal abyss of real Being.
Existence, or God, is not a relation, or a part, but the whole.   Being is
the vast affirmative, excluding negation, self-balanced, and
swallowing up all relations, parts, and times, within itself.   Nature,
truth, virtue, are the influx from thence.   Vice is the absence or
departure of the same.   Nothing, Falsehood, may indeed stand as the
great Night or shade, on which, as a background, the living universe
paints itself forth ; but no fact is begotten by it ; it cannot work ; for it
is not.   It cannot work any good ; it cannot work any harm.   It is
harm, inasmuch as it is worse not to be than to be.

We feel defrauded of the retribution due to evil acts, because the
criminal adheres to his vice and contumacy, and does not come to a
crisis or judgement anywhere in visible nature.   There is no stunning
confutation of his nonsense before men and angels.   Has he therefore
outwitted the law ?   Inasmuch as he carries the malignity and the lie
with him, he so far deceases from nature.   In some manner there will
be a demonstration of the wrong to the understanding also ; but should
we not see it, this deadly deduction makes square the eternal account.

Neither can it be said, on the other hand, that the gain of rectitude
must be bought by any loss.   There is no penalty to virtue ; no penalty
to wisdom ; they are proper additions of being.   In a virtuous action, I
properly *am* ; in a virtuous act, I add to the world ; I plant into deserts
conquered from Chaos and Nothing, and see the darkness receding on
the limits of the horizon.   There can be no excess to love, none to
knowledge, none to beauty, when these attributes are conquered in the

purest sense. The soul refuses all limits. It affirms in man always an Optimism, never a Pessimism.

His life is a progress, and not a station. His instinct is trust. Our instinct uses " more " and " less " in application to man, always of the *presence of the soul*, and not of its absence : the brave man is greater than the coward ; the true, the benevolent, the wise, is more a man, and not less, than the fool and knave. There is, therefore, no tax on the good of virtue ; for that is the incoming of God himself, or absolute existence, without any comparative. All external good has its tax ; and if it came without desert or sweat, has no root in me, and the next wind will blow it away. But all the good of nature is the soul's, and may be had, if paid for in nature's lawful coin, that is, by labour, which the heart and the head allow. I no longer wish to meet a good I do not earn—for example, to find a pot of buried gold—knowing that it brings with it new responsibility. I do not wish more external goods, —neither possessions, nor honours, nor powers, nor persons. The gain is apparent, the tax is certain. But there is no tax on the knowledge that the compensation exists, and that it is not desirable to dig up treasure. Herein I rejoice with a serene eternal peace. I contract the boundaries of possible mischief. I learn the wisdom of St. Bernard : " Nothing can work me damage except myself ; the harm that I sustain, I carry about with me, and never am a real sufferer but by any own fault. "

In the nature of the soul is the compensation for the inequalities of condition. The radical tragedy of nature seems to be the distinction of More and Less. How can Less not feel the pain ; how not feel indignation or malevolence towards More ? Look at those who have less faculty, and one feels sad, and knows not well what to make of it. Almost he shuns their eye ; almost he fears they will upbraid God. What should they do ? It seems a great injustice. But face the facts, and see them nearly, and these mountainous inequalities vanish. Love redoes them all, as the sun melts the iceberg in the sea. The heart and soul of all men being one, this bitterness of *His* and *Mine* ceases. His

is mine. I am my brother, and my brother is me. If I feel
overshadowed and outdone by great neighbours, I can yet love ; I can
still receive ; and he that loveth maketh his own the grandeur he loves.
Thereby I make the discovery that my brother is my guardian, acting
for me with the friendliest designs, and the estate I so admired and
envied is my own. It is the eternal nature of the soul to appropriate
and make all things its own. Jesus and Shakespeare are fragments of
the soul, and by love I conquer and incorporate them in my own
conscious domain. His virtue,—is not that mine ? His wit—if it
cannot be made mine, it is not wit.

Such also, is the natural history of calamity. The changes which
break up at short intervals the prosperity of men are advertisements of
a nature whose law is growth. Evermore it is the order of nature to
grow, and every soul is by this intrinsic necessity putting its whole
system of things, its friends, and home, and laws, and faith, as the
shell-fish crawls out of its beautiful but stony case, because it no
longer admits of its growth, and slowly forms a new house. In
proportion to the vigour of the individual, these revolutions are
frequent, until in some happier mind they are incessant, and all
worldly relations hang very loosely about him, becoming, as it were, a
transparent fluid membrane through which the form is alway seen, and
not, as in most men, an indurated heterogenous fabric of many dates,
and of no settled character, in which the man is imprisoned. Then
there can be no enlargement, and the man of to-day scarcely
recognises the man of yesterday. And such should be the outward
biography of man in time, —a putting off of dead circumstances day
by day, as he renews his raiment day by day. But to us, in our lapsed
estate, resting not advancing, resisting not co-operating with he divine
expansion, this growth comes by shocks.

We cannot part with our friends. We cannot let our angels go. We
do not see that they only go out that archangels may come in. We are
idolators of the Old. We do not believe in the riches of the soul, in its
proper eternity and omnipresence. We do not believe there is any

force in to-day to rival or re-create that beautiful yesterday. We linger in the ruins of the old tent, where we had bread and shelter and organs, nor believe that the spirit can feed, cover, and never us again. We cannot again find aught so dear, so sweet, so graceful. But we sit and weep in vain. The voice of the Almighty saith, " Up and onward for evermore ! " We cannot stay amid the ruins. Neither will we rely on the New : and so we walk with reverted eyes, like these monsters who look backwards.

And yet the compensations of calamity are made apparent to the understanding also, after long intervals of time. A fever, a mutilation, a cruel disappointment, a loss of wealth, a loss of friends, seems at the moment unpaid loss, and unpayable. But the sure years reveal the deep remedial force that underlies all facts. The death of a dear friend, wife, brother, lover, which seemed nothing but privation, somewhat later assumes the aspect of a guide or genius ; for it commonly operates revolutions in our way of life, terminates an epoch of infancy or of youth which was waiting to be closed, breaks up a wonted occupation, or a household, or style of living, and allows the formation of new ones more friendly to the growth of character. It permits or constrains the formation of new acquaintances, and the reception of new years ; and the man or woman who would have remained a sunny garden-flower, with no room for its roots, and too much sunshine for its head, by the falling of the walls and the neglect of the gardener, is made the banian of the forest, yielding shade and fruit to wide neighbourhoods of men.

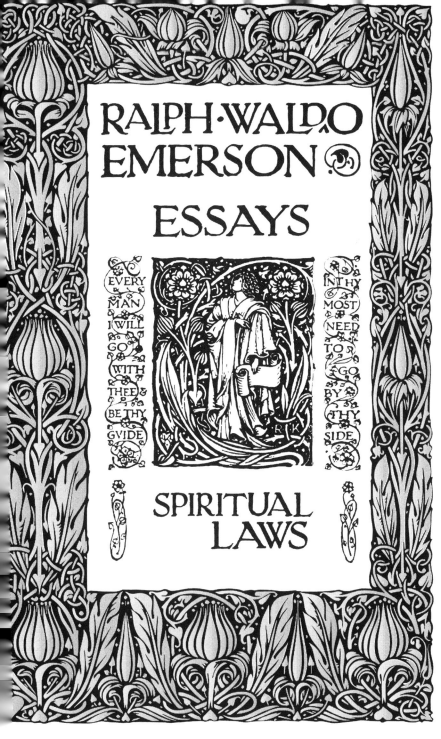

RALPH·WALDO
EMERSON

ESSAYS

EVERY MAN I WILL GO WITH THEE & BE THY GVIDE

INTHY MOST NEED TO GO BY THY SIDE

SPIRITUAL
LAWS

SPIRITUAL LAWS

Edited by A.D Hendry
Cover Art by A.D Hendry

When the act of reflection takes place in the mind, when we look at ourselves in the light of thought, we discover that our life is embosomed in beauty.   Behind us, as we go, all things assume pleasing forms, as clouds do far off.   Not only things familiar and stale, but even the tragic and terrible are comely, as they take their place in the pictures of memory.   The river-bank, the weed at the water-side, the old house, the foolish person,—however neglected in the passing,—have a grace in the past.   Even a corpse that has lain in the chambers has added a solemn ornament to the house.   The soul will not know either deformity or pain.   If in the hours of clear reason we should speak the severest truth, we should say, that we had never made a sacrifice.   In these hours the mind seems so great, that nothing can be taken from us that seems much.   All loss, all pain is particular : the universe remains to the heart unhurt.   Distress never, trifles never abate our trust.   No man ever stated his griefs as lightly as he might. Allow for exaggeration in the most patient and sorely ridden hack that ever was driven.   For it is only the finite that has wrought and suffered ; the infinite lies stretched in smiling repose.

The intellectual life may be kept clean and healthful, if man will live the life of nature, and not import into his mind difficulties which are none of his.   No man need be perplexed in his speculations.   Let him do and say what strictly belongs to him, and though very ignorant of books, his nature shall not yield him any intellectual obstructions and doubts.   Our young people are diseased with the theological problems of original sin, origin of evil, predestination, and the like. These never presented a practical difficulty to any man,—never darkened across any man's road, who did not go out of his way to seek them.   These are the souls mumps and measles and whooping-coughs ; and those who have not caught them cannot describe their health or prescribe the cure.   A simple mind will not know these enemies.   It is quite another thing that he should be able to give account of his faith, and expound to another theory of his self-union and freedom.   This requires rare gifts.   Yet without this self-

knowledge, there may be a sylvan strength and integrity in that which
he is. " A few strong instincts and a few plain rules" suffice us.

My will never gave the images in my mind the rank they now take.
The regular course of studies, the years of academical and professional
education, have not yielded me better facts than some idles books
under the bench at Latin school.   What we do not call education is
more precious than that which we call so.   We form no guess at the
time of receiving a thought, of its comparative value.   And education
often wastes its effort in attempts to thwart and baulk this natural
magnetism, which with sure discrimination selects its own.

In like manner, our moral nature is vitiated by any interference of
our will.   People represent virtue as a struggle, and take to themselves
great airs upon their attainments ; and the question is everywhere
vexed, when a noble nature is commended, Whether the man is not
better who strives with temptation ?   But there is no merit in the
matter.   Either God is there, or he is not there.   We love characters in
proportion as they are impulsive and spontaneous.   The less a man
thinks or knows about his virtues the better we like him.   Timoleon's
victories are the best victories ; which ran and flowed like Homer's
verses, Plutarch said.   When we see a soul whose acts are regal,
graceful, and pleasant as roses, we must thank God that such things
can be and are, and not turn sourly on the angel, and say, " Crump is a
better man with his grunting resistance to all his native devils."

Not less conspicuous is the preponderance of nature over will in all
practical life.   There is less intention in history than we ascribe to it.
We impute deep-laid, far-sighted plans to Cæsar and Napoleon ; but
the best of their power was in nature, not in them.   Men of an
extraordinary success, in their honest moments have always sung,
" Not unto us, not unto us."   According to the faith of their times, they
have built alters to Fortune or to Destiny, or to St. Julian.   Their
success lay in their parallelism to the course of thought, which found
in them an unobstructed channel ; and the wonder of which they were
the visible conductors seemed to the eye their deed.   Did the wires

generate galvanism ?   It is even true that there was less in them on which they could reflect than in another ; as the virtue of a pipe is to be smooth and hollow.   That which externally seemed will and immovableness, was willingness and self-annihilation.   Could Shakespeare give a theory of Shakespeare ?   Could ever a man of prodigious mathematical genius convey to others any insight into his methods ?   If he could communicate that secret, instantly it would lose all its exaggerated value, blending with the daylight and the vital energy, the power to stand and go.

The lesson is forcibly taught by these observations, that our life might be much easier and simpler than we make it ; that the world might be a happier place than it is ; that there is no need of struggles, convulsions, and despairs, of the wringing of the hands and the gnashing of the teeth ; that we miscreate our own evils.   We interfere with the optimism of nature ; for, whenever we get this vantage-ground of the past, or of a wiser mind in the present, we are able to discern that we are begirt with spiritual laws which execute themselves.

The face of external nature teaches the same lesson with calm superiority.   Nature will not have us fret and fume.   She does not like our benevolence or our learning, much better than she likes our frauds and wars.   When we come out of the caucus, or the bank, or the Abolition-convention, or the Temperance-meeting, or the Transcendental club, into the fields and woods, she says to us, " So hot ?   my little sir."

We are full of mechanical actions.   We must needs intermeddle, and have things in our own way, until the sacrifices and virtues of society are odious.   Love should make joy ; but our benevolence is unhappy.   Our Sunday-schools, and churches, and pauper-societies, are yokes to the neck.   We pain ourselves to please nobody.   There are natural ways of arriving at the same ends at which these aim, but do not arrive.   Why should all virtue work in one and the same way ?   Why should all give dollars ?   It is very inconvenient to us country folk, and we do not think any good will come of it.   We have not

dollars. Merchants have : let them give them. Farmers will give
corn. Poets will sing. Women will sew. Labourers will lend a hand.
The children will bring flowers. And why drag this dead weight of a
Sunday school over the Christendom ? It is natural and beautiful that
childhood should inquire, and maturity should teach ; but it is time
enough to answer questions when they are asked. Do not shut up the
young people against their will in a pew, and force the children to ask
them questions for an hour against their will.

If we look wider, things are all alike ; laws, and letters, and creeds,
and modes of living, seem a travesty of truth. Our society is
encumbered by ponderous machinery, which resembles the endless
aqueducts which the Romans built over hill and dale, and which are
suspended by the discovery of the law that water rises to the level of
its source. It is a Chinese wall, which any nimble tartar can leap over.
It is a standing army, not so good as a peace. It is a graduated, titled,
richly appointed Empire, quite superfluous when Town-meetings are
found to answer just as well.

Let us draw a lesson from nature, which always works by short
ways. When the fruit is ripe, it falls. When the fruit is dispatched,
the leaf falls. The circuit of the water is mere falling. The walking of
man and all animals is a falling forward. All our manual labour and
works of strength, as prying, spitting, digging, rowing, and so forth,
are done by dint of continual falling ; and the globe, earth, moon,
comet, sun, star, fall forever and ever.

The simplicity of the universe is very different from the simplicity
of a machine. He who sees moral nature out and out, and thoroughly
knows how knowledge is acquired and character formed, is a pedant.
The simplicity of nature is not that which may easily be read, but is
inexhaustible. The last analysis can no wise be made. We judge of a
man's wisdom by his hope, knowing that the perception of the
inexhaustibleness of nature is an immortal youth. The wild fertility of
nature is felt in comparing our rigid names and reputations with our
fluid consciousness. We pass in the world for sects and schools, for

erudition and piety ; and we are all the time jejune babies. One sees
very well how Pyrrhonism grew up. Every man sees that he is that
middle point whereof everything may be affirmed and denied with
equal reason. He is old, he is young, he is very wise, he is altogether
ignorant. He hears and feels what you say of the seraphim and the tin-
peddler. There is no permanent wise man, except in the figment of the
stoics. We side with the hero, as we read or paint, against the coward
and the robber, and shall be again, not in the low circumstance, but in
comparison with the grandeurs possible to the soul.

A little consideration of what takes place around us every day
would shew us that a higher law than that of our will regulates events ;
that our painful labours are very unnecessary, and altogether fruitless ;
that only in our easy, simple, spontaneous action are we strong, and by
contenting ourselves with obedience we become divine. Belief and
love,—a believing love will relieve us of a vast load of care. O my
brothers, God exists. There is a soul at the centre of nature, and over
the will of every man, so that none of us can wrong the universe. It
has so infused its strong enchantment into nature, that we prosper
when we accept its advice ; and when we struggle to wound its
creatures, our hands are glued to our sides, or they beat our own
breasts. The whole course of things goes to teach us faith. We need
only obey. There is guidance for each of us, and by lowly listening
we shall hear the right word. Why need you choose so painfully your
place, and occupation, and associates, and modes of action and of
entertainment ? Certainly there is a possible right for you, that
precludes the need of balance and wilful election. For you there is a
reality, a fit place and congenial duties. Place yourself in the middle
of the stream of power and wisdom which flows into you as life, place
yourself in the full centre of that flood, then you are without effort
impelled to truth, to right, and a perfect contentment. Then you put all
gainsayers in the wrong. Then you are the world, the measure of
right, of truth, of beauty. If we will not be marplots with our
miserable interferences, the work, the society, letters, arts, science,
religion of men, would go on far better than now ; and the Heaven

predicted from the beginning of the world, and still predicted from the bottom of the heart, would organise itself, as do now the rose and the air and the sun.

I say, *do not choose* ; but that is a figure of speech by which I would distinguish what is commonly called *choice* among men, and which is a partial act, the choice of the hands, of the eye, of the appetites, and not a whole act of the man.   But that which I call right or goodness, is the choice of my constitution ; and that which I call heaven, and inwardly aspire after, is the state or circumstance desirable to my constitution ; and the action which I in all my years tend to do, is the work for my faculties.   We must hold a man amenable to reason for the choice of his daily craft of profession.   It is not an excuse any longer for his deeds that they are the custom for his trade.   What business has he with an evil trade ?   Has he not a *calling* in his character ?

Each man has his own vocation.   The talent is the call.   There is one direction in which all space is open to him.   He has faculties silently inviting him thither to endless exertion.   He is like a ship in a river ; he runs against obstructions on every side but one ; on that side, all obstruction is taken away, and he sweeps serenely over God's depths into an infinite sea.   This talent and this call depend on his organisation, or the mode in which the general soul incarnates itself in him.   He inclines to do something which is easy to him, and good when it is done, but which no other man can do.   He has no rival.   For the more truly he consults his own powers, the more difference will his work exhibit from the work of any other.   When he is true and faithful, his ambition is exactly proportioned to his powers.   The height of the pinnacle is determined by the breadth of the base.   Every man has this call of the power to do somewhat unique, and no man has any other call.   The pretence that he has another call, a summons by name and personal election and outward " sign that mark him extraordinary, and not in the roll of common men," is fanaticism, and betrays obtuseness to perceive that there is one mind in all the individuals, and no respect of persons therein.

By doing his work, he makes the need felt which he can supply. He created the taste by which he is enjoyed. He provokes the wants to which he can minister. By doing his own work, he unfolds himself. It is the vice of our public speaking, that it has not abandonment. Somewhere, not only every orator, but every man, should let out all the length of all the reins ; should find or make a frank and hearty expression of what force and meaning is in him. The common experience is, that the man fits himself as well as he can to the customary details of that work or trade he falls into, and tends it as a dog turns a spit. Then he is a part of the machine he moves ; the man is lost. Until he can manage to communicate himself to others in his full stature and proportion as a wise and good man, he does not yet find his vocation. He must find in that an outlet for his character, so that he may justify himself to their eyes for doing what he does. If the labour is trivial, let him by his thinking and character make it liberal. Whatever he knows and thinks, whatever in his apprehension is worth doing, that let him communicate, or men will never know and honour him aright. Foolish, whenever you take the meanness and formality of that thing you do, instead of converting it into the obedient spiracle of your character and aims.

We only like such actions as have already long had the praise of men ; and do not perceive that any thing man can do may be divinely done. We think greatness entailed or organised in some places or duties, in certain offices or occasions ; and do not see that Paganini can extract rapture from a catgut, and Eulenstein from a jews-harp, and a nimble-fingered lad out of shreds of paper with his scissors, and Landseer out of swine, and the hero out of the pitiful inhibition and company in which he was hidden. What we call obscure condition or vulgar society, is that condition and society whose poetry is not yet written, but which you shall presently make as enviable and renowned as any. Accept your genius, and say what you think. In our estimates, let us take a lesson from kings.   The parts of hospitality, the connexion of families, the impressiveness of death, and a thousand other things, royalty makes its own estimate of, and a royal mind will. To make habitually a new estimate,—that is elevation.

What a man does, that he has.   What has he to do with hope and fear ?   In himself is his might.   Let him regard no good as solid but that which is in his nature, and which must grow out of him as long as he exists.   The goods of fortune may come and go like summer leaves ; let him play with them, and scatter them on every wind, as the momentary signs of his infinite productiveness.

He may have his own.   A man's genius, the quality that differences him from every other, the susceptibility to one class of influences, the selection of what is fit for him, the rejection of what is unfit, determines for him the character of the universe.   As a man thinketh, so is he ; and as a man chooseth, so is he and so is nature.   A man is a method, a progressive arrangement ; a selecting principle, gathering his like to him, wherever he goes.   He takes only his own, out of the multiplicity that sweeps and circles round him.   He is like one of those booms which are set out from the shore on rivers to catch drift-wood, or like the loadstone amongst splinters of steel.

Those facts, words, persons, which dwell in his memory without his being able to say why, remain, because they have a relation to him not less real for being as yet un-apprehended.   They are symbols of value to him, as they can interpret parts of his consciousness which he would vainly seek words for in conventional images of books and other minds.   What attracts my attention shall have it ; as I will go to the man who knocks at my door, whilst a thousand persons, as worthy, go by it, to whom I give no regard.   It is enough that these particulars speak to me.   A few anecdotes, a few traits of character, manners, face, a few incidents, have an emphasis in your memory out of all proportion to their apparent significance, if you measure them by the ordinary standards.   They relate to your gift.   Let them have their weight, and do no reject them, and cast about for illustration and facts more usual in literature. Respect them, for they have their origin in deepest nature. What your heart thinks great, is great. The soul's emphasis is always right.

Over all things that are agreeable to his nature and genius the man has the highest right. Everywhere he may take what belongs to his spiritual estate, nor can he take anything else, though all doors were open, nor can all the force of men hinder him from taking so much. It is vain to attempt to keep a secret from one who has a right to know it. It will tell itself. That mood into which a friend can bring us is his dominion over us. To the thoughts of that state of mind he has a right. All the secrets of that state of mind he can compel. This is a law which statesman use in practice. All the terrors of the French Republic, which held Austria in awe, were unable to command her diplomacy. But Napoleon sent to Vienna M. de Narbonne, one of he old noblesse, with the morals, manners, and name of that interest, saying that it was indispensable to the old aristocracy of Europe men of the same connexion, which, in fact, constitutes a sort of freemasonry. M. Narbonne in less than a fortnight penetrated all the secrets of the Imperial Cabinet.

A mutual understanding is ever the firmest chain. Nothing seems so easy as to speak and to be understood. Yet a man may come to find *that* the strongest of defences and of ties,—that he has been understood ; and he who has received an opinion may come to find it the most inconvenient of bonds.

If a teacher have any opinion which he wishes to conceal, his pupils will become as fully indoctrinated into that as into any which he publishes. If you pour water into a vessel twisted into coils and angles, it is vain to say, I will pour it only into this or that ;—it will find its own level in all. Men feel and act the consequences of your doctrine, without being able to shew how they follow. Shew us an arc of the curve, and a good mathematician will find out the whole figure. We are always reasoning from the seen to the unseen. Hence the perfect intelligence that subsists between wise men of remote ages. A man cannot bury his meanings so deep in his book, but time and like-minded men will find them. Plato had a secret doctrine, had he ? What secret can he conceal from the eyes of Bacon ? of Montaigne? Kant ? Therefore Aristotle said of his works, " they are published and not published."

No man can learn what he has not preparation for learning, however near to his eyes is the object. A chemist may tell his most precious secrets to a carpenter, and he shall never be the wiser,—the secrets he would not utter to a chemist for an estate. God screens us evermore from premature ideas. Our eyes are holden that we cannot see things that stare us in the face, until the hour arrives when the mind is ripened,—then we behold them, and the time when we saw them not is like a dream.

Not in nature but in man is all the beauty and worth he sees. The world is very empty, and is indebted to this gliding, exalting soul for all its pride. " Earth fills her lap with splendours" *not her own.* The vale of Tempe, Tivoli, and Rome, are earth and water, rocks and sky. There are as good earth and water in a thousand places, yet how unaffecting !

People are not the better for the sun and moon, the horizon and the trees ; as it is not observed that the keepers of Roman galleries, or the valets of painters, have any elevation of thought, or that librarians are wiser men than others. There are graces in the demeanour of a polished and noble person, which are lost upon the eye of a churl. These are like the stars whose light has not yet reached us.

He may see what he maketh. Our dreams are the sequel of our waking knowledge. The visions of the night always bear some proportion to the visions of the day. Hideous dreams are only exaggerations of the sins of the day. We see our own evil affections embodied in bad physiognomies. On the Alps, the traveler sometimes sees his own shadow magnified to a giant, so that every gesture of his hand is terrific. " My children," said an old man to his boys scared by a figure in the dark entry, " my children you will never see anything worse than yourselves." As in dreams, so in the scarcely less fluid events of the world, every man sees himself in colossal, without knowing that it is himself that he sees. The good which he sees, compared to the evil which he sees, is as his own good to his own evil. Every quality of his mind is magnified in some one acquaintance, and every emotion of his heart in some one. He is like a quincunx of trees, which counts five, east, west, north, or south ; or an initial, medial, and terminal acrostic. And why not ? He cleaves to one person, and avoids another, according to their likeness or unlikeness to himself, truly seeking himself in his associations, and moreover in his trade, and habits, and gestures, and meats, and drinks ; and comes at last to be faithfully represented by every view you take of his circumstances.

He may read what he writeth. What can we see or acquire, but what we are ? You have seen a skilful man reading Virgil. Well, that author is a thousand books to a thousand persons. Take the book into your two hands, and read your eyes out, you will never find what I find. If any ingenious reader would have a monopoly of the wisdom or delight he gets, he is as secure now the book is Englished, as if it were imprisoned in the Pelews tongue. It is with a good book as it is with good company. Introduce a base person among gentlemen : it is all to no purpose : he is not their fellow. Every society protects itself. The company is perfectly safe, and he is not one of them, though his body is in the room.

What avails it to fight with the eternal laws of mind, which adjust the relation of all persons to each other, by the mathematical measure of their havings and beings ? Gertrude is enamoured of Guy ; how high, how aristocratic, how Roman is mien and manners ! to live with him were life indeed : and no purchase is too great ; and heaven and earth are moved to that end. Well, Gertrude has Guy, but what now avails how high, how aristocratic, how Roman his mien and manners, if his heart and aims are in the senate, in the theatre, and in the billiard-room, and she has no aims, no conversation that can enchant her graceful lord ?

He shall have his own society.   We can love nothing but nature. The most wonderful talents, the most meritorious exertions really avail very little with us ; but nearness or likeness of nature,—how beautiful is the ease of its victory !   Persons approach us famous for their beauty, for their accomplishments, worthy of all wonder for their charms and gifts : they dedicate their whole skill to the hour and the company, with very imperfect results.   To be sure, it would be very ungrateful in us not to praise them very loudly.   Then, when all is done, a person of related mind, a brother or sister by nature, comes to us so softly and easily, so nearly and intimately, as if it were the blood in our proper veins, that we feel as if some one was gone, instead of another having come : we are utterly relieved and refreshed : it is a sort of joyful solitude.   We foolishly think, in our days of sin, that we must court friends by compliance to the customs of society, to its dress, its breeding and its estimates.   But later, if we are so happy, we learn that only that soul can be my friend, which I encounter on the line of my own march, that soul to which I do not decline, and which does not decline to me, but, native of the same celestial latitude, repeats in its own all my experience.   The scholar and the prophet forget themselves, and ape the customs and costumes of the man of the world, to deserve the smile of beauty.   He is a fool, and follows some giddy girl, and not with religious ennobling passion a woman with all that is serene, oracular and beautiful in her soul.   Let him be great, and love shall follow him.   Nothing is more deeply punished than the neglect of the affinities by which alone society should be formed, and the insane levity of choosing associates by others' eyes.

He may set his own rate.   It is an universal maxim, worthy of all acceptation, that a man may have that allowance he takes.   Take the place and attitude to which you see your unquestionable right, and all men acquiesce.   The world might be just.   It always leaves every man with profound unconcern to set his own rate.   Hero or driveller, it meddles not in the matter.   It will certainly accept your own measure of your doing and being, whether you sneak about and deny your own name, or whether you seek your work produced to the concave sphere of the heavens, one with the revolution of the stars.

The same reality pervades all teaching.   The man may teach by doing, and not otherwise.   If he can communicate himself, he can teach, but not by words.   He teaches who gives, and he learns who receives.   There is no teaching until the pupil is brought into the same state or principle in which you are ; a transfusion takes place : he is you, and you are he ; then is a teaching, and by no unfriendly chance or bad company can he ever quite lose the benefit.   But your propositions run out of one ear as they ran in at the other.   We see it advertised that Mr. Grand will deliver an oration on the fourth of July, and Mr. Hand before the Mechanics' Association, and we do not go thither, because we know that these gentlemen will not communicate their own character and being to the audience.   If we had reason to expect such a communication, we should go through all inconvenience and opposition.   The sick would be carried in litters.   But a public oration is an escapade, a non-committal, an apology, a gag, and not a communication, not a speech, not a man.

A like Nemesis presides over all intellectual works.   We have yet to learn that the thing uttered in words is not therefore affirmed.   It must affirm itself, or no forms of grammar and no plausibility can give it evidence, and no array of arguments.   The sentence must also contain its own apology for being spoken.

The effect of any writing on the public mind is mathematically measurable by its depth of thought.   How much water does it draw ? If it awaken you to think ; if it lift you from your feet with the great voice of eloquence ; then the effect is to be wide, slow, permanent, over the minds of men ; if the pages instruct you not, they will die like flies in the hour.   The way to speak and write what shall not go out of fashion, is to speak and write sincerely.   The argument which has not power to reach my own practice, I may well doubt will fail to reach

yours.   But take Sidney's maxim : " Look in thy heart and write."   He
that writes to himself writes to an eternal public.   That statement only
is fit to be made public which you have come at in attempting to
satisfy your own curiosity.   The writer who takes his subject from his
ear and not from his heart, should know that he has lost as much as he
seems to have gained ; and when the empty book has gathered all its
praise, and half the people say—" What poetry ! what genius !" it still
needs fuel to make fire.   That only profits which is profitable.   Life
alone can impart life ; and though we should burst, we can only be
valued as we make ourselves valuable.   There is no luck in literary
reputation.   They who make up the final verdict upon every book, are
not the partial and the noisy readers of the hour when it appears ; but a
court as of angels, a public not to be bribed, not to be entreated, and
not to be overawed, decides upon every man's title to fame.   Only
those books come down which deserve to last.   All the gilt edges and
vellum and morocco, all the presentation-copies to all the libraries,
will not preserve a book in circulation beyond its intrinsic date.   It
must go with all Walpole's Royal and Noble Authors to its fate.
Blackmore, Kotzebue, or Pollok, may endure for a night, but Moses
and Homer stand forever.   There are not in the world at any one time
more than a dozen persons who read and understand Plato :—never
enough to pay for an edition of his works ; yet to every generation
these come duly down, for the sake of those few persons, as if God
brought them in his hand.   " No book," said Bentley, " was ever
written down by any but itself."   The permanence of all books is fixed
by no effort friendly or hostile, but by their won specific gravity, or the
intrinsic importance of their contents to the constant mind of man.
" Do not trouble yourself too much about the light on your statue,"
said Michael Angelo to the young sculptor ; " the light of the public
square will test its value."

In like manner the effect of every action is measured by the depth
of the sentiment from which it proceeds.   The great man knew not that
he was great.   It took a century or two for that fact to appear.   What
he did, he did because he must ; he used no election ; it was the most

natural thing in the world, and grew out of the circumstances of every moment. But now, every thing he did, even to the lifting of his finger, or the eating of bread, looks large, all-related, and is called an institution.

These are the demonstrations, in a few particulars, of the genius of nature : they shew the direction of the stream. But the stream is blood ; every drop is alive. Truth has not single victories ; all things are its organs, not only dust and stones, but errors and lies. The laws of disease, physicians say, are as beautiful as the laws of health. Our philosophy is affirmative, and readily accepts the testimony of negative facts, as every shadow points to the sun. By a divine necessity, every fact in nature is constrained to offer its testimony.

Human character does not evermore publish itself. It will not be concealed. It hates darkness,—it rushes into light. The most fugitive deed and word, the mere air of doing a thing, the intimated purpose, expresses character. If you act, you shew character ; if you sit still, you shew it ; if you sleep, you shew it. You think because you have spoken nothing, when others spoke, and have given no opinion on the times, on the church, on slavery, on the college, on parties and persons, that your verdict is still expected with curiosity as a reserved wisdom. Far otherwise ; your silence answers very loud. You have no oracle to utter, and your fellow men have learned that you cannot help them ; for oracles speak. Doth not wisdom cry, and understanding put forth her voice ?

Dreadful limits are set in nature to the powers of dissimulation. Truth tyrannises over the unwilling members of the body. Faces never lie, it is said. No man need be deceived, who will study the changes of expression. When a man speak the truth in the spirit of truth, his eye is as clear as the heavens. When he has base ends, and speaks falsely, the eye is muddy and sometimes asquint.

I have heard an experienced counsellor say, that he feared never the effect upon a jury of a lawyer who does not believe in his heart that his client ought to have a verdict. If he does not believe it, his unbelief will appear to the jury, despite all his protestations, and will become their unbelief. This is that law whereby a work of art, of whatever kind, sets us in the same state of mind wherein the artist was when he made it. That which we do not believe, we cannot adequately say, though we may repeat the words ever so often. It was this conviction which Swedenborg expressed, when he described a group of persons in the spiritual world endeavouring in vain to articulate a proposition which they did not believe : but they could not, though they twisted and folded their lips even to indignation.

A man passes for that he is worth. Very idle is all curiosity concerning other people's estimate of us, and idle is all fear of remaining unknown. If a man know that he can do any thing,—that he can do it better than any one else,—he has a pledge of the acknowledgement of that fact by all persons. The world is full of judgement-days, and into every assembly that a man enters, in every action he attempts he is gauged and stamped. In every troop of boys that whoop and run in each yard and square, a new-comer is as well and accurately weighed in the balance, in the course of a few days, and stamped with his right number, as if he had undergone a formal trial of his strength, speed, and temper. A stranger comes from a distant school, with better dress, with trinkets in his pockets, with airs, and pretension : an old boy sniffs thereat, and says to himself, " It's of no use : we shall find him out to-morrow." " What hath he done ?" is the divine question which searches men, and transpierces every false reputation. A fop may sit in any chair of the world, nor be distinguished for his hour from Homer and Washington ; but there can never be any doubt concerning the respective ability of human beings, when we seek the truth. Pretension may sit still, but cannot act. Pretension never feigned an act of real greatness. Pretension never wrote an Iliad, nor drove back Xerxes, nor christianised the world, nor abolished slavery.

Always as much virtue as there is, so much appears ; as much goodness as there is, so much reverence it commands. All the devils respect virtue. The high, the generous, the self-devoted sect will always instruct and command mankind. Never a sincere word was utterly lost. Never a magnanimity fell to the ground. Always the heart of man greets and accepts it unexpectedly. A man passes for that he is worth. What he is, engraves itself on his face, on his form, on his fortunes, in letters of light, which all men may read but himself. Concealment avails him nothing ; boasting, nothing. There is confession in the glances of our eyes, in our smiles, in salutations, and the grasp of hands. His sin bedaubs him, mars all his good impression. Men know not why they do not trust him ; but they do not trust him. His vice glasses his eye, demeans his cheek, pinches the nose, sets the mark of the beast on the back of the head, and writes, O fool ! fool ! on the forehead of a king.

If you would not be known to do anything, never do it. A man may play the fool in the drifts of a desert, but every grain of sand shall seem to see. He may be a solitary eater, but he cannot keep his foolish council. A broken complexion, a swinish look, ungenerous acts, and the want of due knowledge,—all blab. Can a cook, a Chiffinch, an Iachhimo, be mistaken for Zeno or Paul ? Confucius exclaimed, " How can a man be concealed ! How can a man be concealed !"

On the other hand, the hero fears not, that if he withhold the avowal of a just and brave act, it will go unwitnessed and unloved. One knows it,—himself,—and is pledged to it by sweetness of peace, and to nobleness of aim, which will prove in the end a better proclamation of it than the relating of the incident. Virtue is the adherence in action to the nature of things, and the nature of things makes it prevalent. It consists in a perpetual substitution of being for seeming, and with sublime propriety God is described as saying, I AM.

The lesson which all these observations convey, is, Be, and not seem. Let us acquiesce. Let us take our bloated nothingness out of the path of divine circuits. Let us unlearn our wisdom of the world.

Let us lie low in the Lord's power, and learn that truth alone makes rich and great.

If you visit your friend, why need you apologise for not having visited him, and waste his time and deface your own act ? Visit him now. Let him feel that the highest love has come to see him, in thee its lowest organ. Or why need you torment yourself and friend by secret self-reproaches that you have not assisted him or complimented him with gifts and salutations heretofore ? Be a gift and a benediction. Shine with real light, and not with borrowed reflections of gifts. Common men are apologies for men ; they bow the head, they excuse themselves with prolix reasons, they accumulate appearances because the substance is not.

We are full of these superstitions of sense, the worship of magnitude. God loveth not size ; whale and minnow are of like dimension. But we call the poet inactive, because he is not a president, a merchant, or a porter. We adore an institution, and do not see that it is founded on a thought which we have. But real action is in silent moments. The epochs of our life are not in the visible facts of our choice of a calling, our marriage, our acquisition of an office, and the like ; but in a silent thought by the way-side as we walk ; in a thought which revises our entire manner of life, and says, " Thus hast thou done, but it were better thus" And all our after years, like menials, do serve and wait on this, and according to their ability do execute its will. This revisal or correction is a constant force, which, as a tendency, reaches through our lifetime. The object of the man, the aim of these moments, is to make daylight shine through him, to suffer the law to traverse his whole being without obstruction, so that, on what point soever of his doing your eye falls, it shall report truly of his character, whether it be his diet, his house, his religious forms, his society, his mirth, his vote, his opposition. Now he is not homogenous, but heterogeneous, and the ray does not traverse ; there are no thorough lights : but the eye of the beholder is puzzled, detecting many unlike tendencies, and a life not yet at one.

Why should we make it a point with our false modesty to disparage that man we are and that form of being assigned to us ? A good man is contented. I love and honour Epaminondas, but I do not wish to be Epaminondas. I hold it more just to love the world of this hour than the world of his hour. Nor can you, if I am true, excite me to the least uneasiness by saying, " he acted, and thou sittest still." I see action to be good, when the need is, and sitting still to be also good. Epaminondas, if he was the man I take him for, would have sat still with joy and peace, if his lot had been mine. Heaven is large, and affords space for all modes of love and fortitude. Why should we be busy-bodies and superservicable ? Action and inaction are alike to the true. One piece of the tree is cut for a weathercock, and one for the sleeper of a bridge ; the virtue of the wood is apparent in both.

I desire not to disgrace the soul. The fact that I am here, certainly shews me that the soul had need of an organ here. Shall I not assume the post ? Shall I skulk and dodge and duck with my unseasonable apologies and vain modesty, and imagine my being here impertinent ? less pertinent than Epaminondas or Homer being there ? and that the soul did not know its own needs ? Besides, without any reasoning on the matter, I have no discontent. The good soul nourishes me alway, unlocks new magazines of power and enjoyment to me every day. I will not meanly decline the immensity of good, because I have heard it has come to others in another shape.

Besides, why should we be cowed by the name of Action ? 'Tis a trick of the senses,—no more. We know that the ancestor of every action is a thought. The poor mind does not seem to itself to be any thing, unless it have an outside badge,—some Gentoo diet, or Quaker coat, or Calvinistic prayer-meeting, or philanthropic society, or a great donation, or a high office, or, any how, some wild contrasting action to testify that it is some-what. The rich mind lies in the sun and sleeps, and is Nature. To think is to act.

Let us, if we must have great actions, make our own so. All action is of an infinite elasticity, and the least admits of being inflated with

the celestial air until it eclipses the sun and moon.   Let us seek *one*
peace by fidelity.   Let me do my duties.   Why need I go gadding into
the scenes and philosophy of Greek and Italian history, before I have
washed my own face, or justified myself to my own benefactors ?
How dare I read Washington's campaigns, when I have not answered
the letters of my own correspondents ?   Is not that a just objection to
much of our reading ?   It is a pusillanimous desertion of our work to
gaze after our neighbours.   It is peeping.   Byron says of Jack Bunting,

> " He knew not what to say, and so he swore."

I may say it of our preposterous use of books : " He knew not what
to do, and so he *read.*"   I can think of nothing to fill my time with, and
so, without any constraint, I find the life of Brant.   It is a very
extravagant compliment to pay to Brant, or to General Schuyler, or to
General Washington.   My time should be as good as their time : my
world, my facts, all my net of relations as good as theirs, or either of
theirs.   Rather let me do my work so well that other idlers, if they
choose, may compare my texture with the texture of these, and find it
identical with the best.

This over-estimate of the possibilities of Paul and Pericles, this
under-estimate of our own, comes from a neglect of the fact of an
identical nature.   Buonaparte knew but one Merit, and rewarded in
one and the same way the good soldier, the good astronomer, the good
poet, the good player.   Thus he signified his sense of a great fact.   The
poet uses the name of Cæsar, of Tamerlane, of Bonduca, of Belisarius ;
the painter uses the conventional story of the Virgin Mary, of Paul, of
Peter.   He does not, therefore, defer to the nature of these accidental
men, of these stock heroes.   If the poet write a true drama, then he is
Cæsar, and not the player of Cæsar ; then the self-same strain of
thought, emotion as pure, wit as subtle, motions as swift, mounting,
extravagant, and a heart as great, self-sufficing, dauntless, which on
the waves of its love and hope can uplift all that is reckoned solid and
precious in the world, palaces, gardens, money, navies, kingdoms,—
marking its own incomparable worth by the sight it casts on these

gauds of men,—these all are his, and by the power of these he rouses the nations. But the great names cannot stead him, if he have not life himself. Let a man believe in God, and not in names and places and persons. Let the great soul incarnated in some woman's form, poor and sad and single, in some Dolly or Joan, go out to service, and sweep chambers and scour floors, and its effulgent day-beams cannot be muffled or hid, but to sweep and scour will instantly appear supreme and beautiful actions, the top and radiance of human life, and all people will get mops and brooms ; until lo, suddenly the great soul has enshrined itself in some other form, and done some other deed, and that is now the floor and head of all living nature.

We are the photometers, we the irritate gold leaf and tinfoil that measure the accumulations of the subtle element. We know the authentic effects of the true fire through every one of its million disguises.

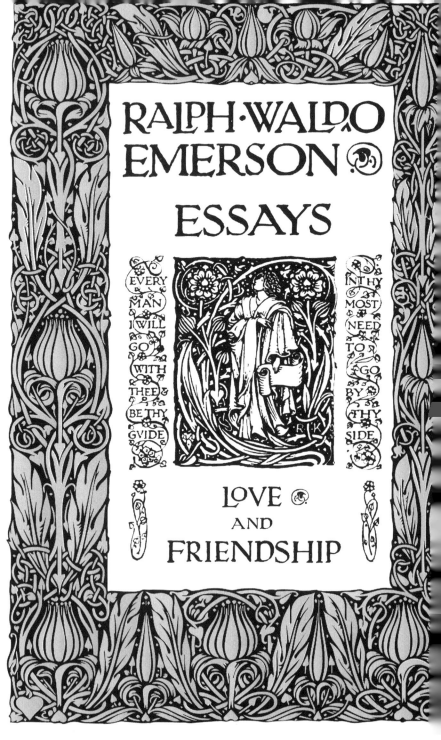

RALPH·WALDO EMERSON

ESSAYS

EVERY MAN I WILL GO WITH THEE & BE THY GVIDE

IN THY MOST NEED TO GO BY THY SIDE

LOVE
AND
FRIENDSHIP

LOVE

Edited by A.D Hendry
Cover Art by A.D Hendry

Every soul is a celestial Venus to every other soul. The heart has its sabbaths and jubilees, in which the world appears as a hymeneal feast, and all natural sounds and the circle of the seasons are erotic odes and dances. Love is omnipresent in nature as motive and reward. Love is our highest word, and the synonym of God. Every promise of the soul has innumerable fulfilments ; each of its joys ripens into new wants. Nature, uncontainable, flowing, forelooking, in the first sentiment of kindness anticipates already a benevolence which shall lose all particular regards in its general light. The introduction of this felicity is in a private and tender relation of one to one, which is the enchantment of human life ; which, like a certain divine rage and enthusiasm, seizes on man at one period and works a revolution in his mind and body ; unites him to his race, pledges him to the domestic and civic relations, carries him with new sympathy into nature, enhances the power of the senses, opens the imagination, adds to his character heroic and sacred attributes, establishes marriage, and gives permanence to human society.

The natural association of the sentiment of love with the heyday of the blood seems to require that in order to portray it in vivid tints, which every youth and maid should confess to be true to their throbbing experience, one must not be too old. The delicious fancies of youth reject the last savour of a mature philosophy, as chilling with age and pedantry their purple bloom. And therefore I know I incur the imputation of unnecessary hardness and stoicism from those who compose the Court and Parliament of Love. But from these formidable censors I shall appeal to my seniors. For it is to be considered, that this passion of which we speak, though it begin with the young, yet forsakes not the old, or rather suffers no one who is truly its servant to grow old, but makes the aged participators of it, not less than the tender maiden, though in a different and nobler sort. For it is a fire that, kindling its first embers in the narrow nook of a private bosom, caught from a wandering spark out of another private heart, glows and enlarges until it warms and beams upon multitudes of men and women, upon the universal heart of all, and so lights up the whole world and all nature with its generous flames. It matters not, therefore, whether we attempt to describe the passion at twenty, at thirty, or at eighty years. He who paints it at the first period will lose some of its later, he who paints it at the last, some of its earlier traits. Only it is to be hoped that, by patience and the Muses' aid, we may attain to that inward view of the law, which shall describe a truth ever young, ever beautiful, so central that it shall commend itself to the eye at whatever angle beholden.

And the first condition is, that we must leave a too close and lingering adherence to the actual, to facts, and study the sentiment as it appeared in hope and not in history. For each man sees his own life defaced and disfigured, as the life of man is not, to his imagination. Each man sees over his own experience a certain slime of error, whilst that of other men looks fair and ideal. Let any man go back to those delicious relations which make the beauty of his life, which have given him sincerest instruction and nourishment, he will shrink and shrink. Alas ! I know not why, but bitter compunctions embitter in mature life all the remembrances of budding sentiment, and cover every beloved name. Every thing is beautiful seen from the point of intellect, or as truth. But all is sour, if seen as experience. Details are always melancholy ; the plan is seemly and noble. It is strange how painful is the actual world, —the painful kingdom of time and place. There dwells care and canker and fear. With thought, with the ideal, is immortality hilarity, the rose of joy. Round it all Muses sing. But with names and persons, and the partial interest of today and yesterday, is grief.

The strong bent of nature is seen in the proportion which this topic of personal relations usurps in the conversation of society. What do we wish to know of any worthy person so much as how he has sped in the history of this sentiment ? What books in the circulating libraries circulate ? How we glow over these novels of passion, when the story is told with any spark of truth and nature ! And what fastens attention, in the intercourse of life, like any passage betraying affection between

two parties ?   Perhaps we never saw them before, and shall never see
them again.   But we see them exchange a glance, or betray a deep
emotion, and we are no longer strangers.   We understand them, and
take the warmest interest in the development of the romance.   All
mankind love a lover.   The earliest demonstration of complacency and
kindness are nature's most winning pictures.   It is the dawn of civility
and grace in the coarse and rustic.   The rude village boy teases the
girls about the school-house door ;—but today he comes running into
the entry, and meets one fair child arranging her satchel ; he holds her
books to help her, and instantly it seems to him as if she removed
herself from him infinitely, and was a sacred precinct.   Among the
throng of girls he runs rudely enough, but one alone distances him :
and these two little neighbours, that were so close just now, have
learned to respect each other's personality.   Or who can avert his eyes
from the engaging, half-artful, half-artless ways of schoolgirls who go
into the country shops to buy a skein of silk or a sheet of paper, and
talk half an hour about nothing with the broad-faced, good-natured
shop-boy ?   In the village they are on a perfect equality, which love
delights in, and without any coquetry, the happy, affectionate nature of
woman flows out in this pretty gossip.   The girls may have little
beauty, yet plainly do they establish between them and the good boy
the most agreeable, confiding relations, what with their fun and their
earnest, about Edgar, and Jonas, and Almira, and who was invited to
the party, and who was danced at the dancing school, and when the
singing school would begin, and other nothings concerning which the
parties cooed.   By and by the boy wants a wife, and very truly and
heartily will he know where to find a sincere and sweet mate, without
any risk such as Milton deplores as incident to scholars and great men.

   I have been told that my philosophy is unsocial, and that in public
discourses, my reverence for the intellect makes me unjustly cold to
the personal relations.   But now I almost shrink at the remembrance of
such disparaging words.   For persons are love's world, and the coldest
philosopher cannot recount the debt of the young soul wandering here
in nature to the power of love, without being tempted to unsay, as

treasonable to nature, aught derogatory to the social instincts.   For, though the celestial rapture falling out of heaven seizes only upon those of tender age, and although a beauty overpowering all analysis or comparison, and putting us quite beside ourselves, we can seldom see after thirty years, yet the remembrances of these visions outlasts all other remembrances, and is a wreath of flowers on the oldest brows. But here is a strange fact, it may seem to many men, in revising their experience, that they have no fairer page in their life's book than the delicious memory of some passages wherein affection contrived to give a witchcraft surpassing the deep attraction of its own truth to a parcel of accidental and trivial circumstances.   In looking backward, they may find that several things which were not the charm have more reality to this groping memory than the charm itself which embalmed them.   But be our experience in particulars what it may, no man ever forgot the visitations of that power to his heart and brain, which created all things new ; which was the dawn in him of music, poetry, and art ; which made the face of nature radiant with purple light, the morning and the night varied enchantments ; when a single tone of one voice could make the heart beat, and the most trivial circumstances associated with one form is put in the amber of memory ; when we became all eye when one was present, and all memory when one was gone, when the youth becomes a watcher of windows, and studious of a glove, a veil, a ribbon, or the wheels of a carriage ; when no place is too solitary and none too silent for him who has richer company and sweeter conversation in his new thoughts than any old friends, though best and purest, can give him ; for the figures, the motions, the words of the beloved object are not like the other images written in water, but, as Plutarch said, "enamelled in fire," and makes the study of midnight.

"Thou art not gone being gone, where'er thou art ;

thou leav'st in him thy watchful eyes, in him thy loving heart."

In the noon and the afternoon of life we still throb at the recollection of days when happiness was not happy enough, but must be drugged with the relish of pain and fear ; for he touched the secret of the matter who said of love,

" All other pleasures are not worth its pains :"

and when the day was not long enough, but the night too must be consumed in keen recollections ; when the head boiled all night on the pillow with generous deed it resolved on ; when the moonlight was a pleasing fever, and the stars were letters, and the flowers ciphers, and the air was coined into song ; when all business seems an impertinence, and all the men and women running to and fro in the streets mere pictures.

The passion remakes the world for the youth. It makes all things alive and significant. Nature grows conscious. Every bird on the boughs of the tree sings now to his heart and soul. Almost the notes are articulate. The clouds have faces as he looks on them. The trees of the forest, the waving grass, and the peeping flowers, have grown intelligent ; and almost he fears to trust them with the secret which they seem to invite. Yet natures soothes and sympathises. In the green solitude he finds a dearer home than with men.

" Fountain-heads and pathless groves,

Places which pale passion loves,

Moonlight walks, when all the fowls

Are safely housed, save bats and owls,

A midnight bell, a passing groan, —

These are the sounds we feed upon."

Behold there in the wood the fine madman ! He is a palace of sweet sounds and sights ; he dilates ; he is twice a man ; he walks with his arms akimbo ; he soliloquises ; he accuses the grass and the trees ; he feels the blood of the violet, the clover and the lily, in his veins ; and he talks with the brook that wets his foot.

The causes that have sharpened his perceptions of natural beauty have made him love music and verse.   It is a fact often observed, that men have written good verses under the inspiration of passion, who cannot write well under any other circumstances.

The like force has the passion over all his nature.   It expands the sentiment ; it makes the clown gentle, and gives the coward heart. Into the most pitiful and abject it will infuse a heart and courage to defy the world, so only it have the countenance of the beloved object. In giving him to another, it still gives more him to himself.   He is a new man, with new perceptions and keener purposes, and a religious solemnity of character and aims.   He does not longer appertain to his family and society.   *He* is somewhat.   *He* is a person.   *He* is a soul.

And here let us examine a little nearer the nature of that influence which is thus potent over the human youth. Let us approach and admire Beauty, whose revelation to man we now celebrate,—beauty, welcome as the sun wherever it pleases to shine, which pleases everybody with it and with themselves. Wonderful is its charm. It seems sufficient to itself. The lover cannot paint the maiden to his fancy poor and solitary. Like a tree in flower, so much soft, budding, informing loveliness is society for itself, and she teaches this eye why beauty was ever painted with Loves and Graces attending her steps. Her existence makes the world rich. Though she excludes all other persons from his attention as cheap and unworthy, yet she indemnifies him by carrying out her own being into somewhat impersonal, large, mundane, so that the maiden stands to him for a representative of all select things and virtues. For that reason the lover sees never personal resemblances in his mistress to her kindred or to others. His friends find in her a likeness to her mother, or her sisters, or to persons not of her blood. The lover sees no resemblance except to summer evenings and diamond mornings, to rainbows and the song of birds.

Beauty is ever that divine things the ancients esteemed it. It is, they said, the flowering of virtue. Who can analyse the nameless charm which glands from one and another face and form ? We are touched with emotions of tenderness and complacency, but we cannot find whereat this dainty emotion, this wandering gleam points. It is destroyed for the imagination by any attempt to defer it to organisation. Nor does it point to any relations of friendship or love that society knows and has ; but, as it seems to me, to a quite other and unattainable sphere, to relations of transcendent delicacy and sweetness, a true faerie land ; to what roses and violets hint and foreshew. We cannot get at beauty. Its nature is like opaline doves'-neck lustres, hovering and evanescent. Herein it resembles the most excellent things, which all have this rainbow character, defying all attempts at appropriation and use. What else did Jean Paul Richter signify, when he said to music, " Away ! away ! thou speaks to me of things which in all my endless life I have found not, and shall not find." The same fact may be observed in every work of the plastic arts. The statue then beautiful, when it begins to be incomprehensible, when it is passing out of criticism, and can no longer be defined by compass and measuring wand, but demands an active imagination go with it, and to say what it is in the act of doing. The god or hero of the sculptor is always represented in a transition *from* that which is representable to the sense, *to* that which is not. Then first it ceases to be a stone. The same remark holds of painting. And of poetry, the success is not attained when it lulls and satisfies, but when it astonishes and fires us with new endeavours after the unattainable. Concerning it, Landor inquires " whether it is not to be referred to some purer state of sensation and existence." So it must be with personal beauty, which love worships. Then first it is charming and itself, when it dissatisfies us with any end ; when it becomes a story without an end ; when it suggests gleams and visions, and not earthly satisfactions ; when it seems

> " too bright and good

> For human nature's daily food" ;

when it makes the beholder feel his unworthiness ; then he cannot feel his right to it, though he were Cæsar ; he cannot feel more right to it than to the firmament and the splendours of a sunset.

Hence arose the saying, " If I love you, what is that to you ?" We say so, because we feel that what we love is not within your will, but above it. It is the radiance of you, and not you. It is that which you know not in yourself, and can never know.

This agrees well with that high philosophy of Beauty which the ancient writers delighted in ; for they said, that the soul of a man, embodied here on earth, went roaming up and down in quest of that other world of its own, out of which it came into this, but was soon stupefied by the light of the natural sun, and unable to see any other objects that those of this world, which are but shadows of real things. Therefore the Deity sends the glory of youth before the soul, that it may avail itself of beautiful bodies as aids to its recollection of the celestial good and fair ; and the man beholding such a person in the female sex, runs to her, and finds the highest joy in contemplating the form, movement, and intelligence of this person, because it suggests to him the presence of that which indeed is within the beauty, and the cause of the beauty.

If, however, from too much conversing with material objects, the soul was gross, and misplaced its satisfaction in the body, it reaped nothing but sorrow ; body being unable to fulfil the promise which beauty holds out ; but if, accepting the hint of these visions and suggestions which beauty makes to his mind, the soul passes through the body, and falls to admire strokes of character, and the lovers contemplate one another in their discourses and their actions, they pass to the true palace of Beauty, more and more inflame their love of it, and by this love extinguishing the base affection, as the sun puts out the fire by shining on the hearth, they become pure and hallowed. By conversation with that which is in itself excellent, magnanimous, lowly, and just, the lover comes to a warmer love of these nobilities, and a quicker apprehension of them. Then he passes from loving them in one, to loving them in all ; and so is the one beautiful soul only the door through which he enters to society of his mate he attains a clearer sight of any spot, any taint, which her beauty has contracted from this world, and is able to point it out, and this with mutual joy that they are now able without offence to indicate blemishes and hinderances in each other, and give to each all help and comfort in curing the same. And, beholding in many souls the traits of the divine beauty, and separating in each soul that which is divine from the taint which they have contracted in the world, the lover ascends ever to the highest beauty, to the love and knowledge of the Divinity, by steps on this ladder of created souls.

Somewhat like this have the truly wise told us of love in all ages. The doctrine is not old, nor is it new. If Plato, Plutarch, and Apuleius, taught it, so have Petrarch, Angelo, and Milton. It awaits a truer unfolding, in opposition and rebuke to that subterranean prudence which presides at marriage with words that take hold of the upper world, whilst one eye is eternally boring down into the cellar, so that its gravest discourse has ever a slight savour of hams and powdering-tubs.   Worst, when the snout of this sensualism intrudes into the education of young women, and withers the hope and affection of human nature, by teaching that marriage signifies nothing but a housewife's thrift, and that woman's life has no other aim.

But in this dream of love, though beautiful, is only one scene in our play.   In the procession of the soul from within outward, it enlarges its circles ever, like the pebble thrown into the pond, or the light proceeding from an orb.   The rays of the soul alight first on the signs nearest, on every utensil and toy, on nurses and domestics, on the house and yard and passengers, on the circle of household acquaintance, on politics, and geography, and history.   But by the necessity of our constitution, things are ever grouping themselves according to higher or more interior laws.   Neighbourhood, size, numbers, habits, persons, lose by degrees their power over us.   Cause and effect, real affinities, the longing for harmony between the soul and circumstance, the high progressive idealising instinct, these predominate later, and ever the step backward from the higher to the lower relations is impossible.   Thus even love, which is the deification of persons, must become more impersonal every day.   Of this at first it gives no hint.   Little think the youth and maiden who are glancing at each other across crowded rooms, with eyes so full of mutual intelligence,—of the precious fruit long hereafter to proceed from this new, quite external stimulus.   The work of vegetation begins first in the irritability of the bark and leaf-buds.   From exchanging glances, they advance to acts of courtesy, of gallantry, then to fiery passion, to plighting troth and marriage.   Passions beholds its object as a perfect unit.   The soul is wholly embodied, and the body is wholly ensouled.

" Her pure and eloquent blood

Spoke in her cheeks, and so distinctly wrought,

That one might almost say her body thought."

Romeo, if dead, should be cut up into little stars to make the heavens fine. Life with this pair, has not other aim, asks no more than Juliet,—than Romeo. Night, day, studies, talents, kingdoms, religion, are all contained in this form full of soul, in this soul which is all form. The lovers delight in endearments, in avowals of love, in comparisons of their regards. When alone, they solace themselves with the remembered image of the other. Does that other see the same star, the same melting cloud, read the same book, feel the same emotion, that now delight me ? They try and weigh their affection, and adding up all costly advantages, friends, opportunities, properties, exult in discovering that willingly, joyfully, they would give us all as a ransom for the beautiful, the beloved head, not one hair of which shall be harmed. But the lot of humanity is on these children. Danger, sorrow, and pain arrive to them, as to us all. Love prays. It makes covenants with Eternal Power, in behalf of this dear mate. The union which is thus effected, and which mutes every thread throughout the whole web of relation into a golden ray, and bathes the soul in a new and sweeter element, —is yet a temporary state. Not always can flowers, pearls poetry, protestations, nor even home in another heart, content the awful soul that dwells in clay. It arouses itself at last from these endearments, as toys, and puts on the harness, and aspires to vast and universal aims. The soul which is in the soul of each, craving for a perfect beatitude, detects incongruities, defects, and disproportion in the behaviour of the other. Hence arises surprise, expostulation, and pain. Yet that which drew them to each other was signs of loveliness, signs of virtue : and these virtues are there, however eclipsed. They appear and reappear, and continue to attract ; but the regard changes, quits the sign, and attaches to the substance. This repairs the wounded affection. Meanwhile, as life wears on, it proves a game of permutation and combination of all possible positions of the parties, to extort the resources of each, and acquaint each with the whole strength and weakness of the other. For it is the nature and end of this relation, that they should represent the human race to each other. All this is in the world which is or ought to be known, is cunningly wrought into the texture of man, of woman.

" The person love does to us fit,

Like manna, has the taste of all in it."

The world rolls : the circumstances vary every hour.   All the
angels that inhabit this temple of the body appear at the windows, and
all the gnomes and vices also.   By all the virtues they are united.   If
there be virtue, all the vices are known as such ; they confess and flee.
Their once flaming regard is sobered by time in either breast, and
losing in violence what it gains inexistent, it becomes a thorough good
understanding.   They resign each other, without complaint, to the
good offices which man and woman are severally appointed to
discharge in time ; and its object, for cheerful, disengaged furtherance,
whether present or absent, of each other's designs.   At last they
discover that all which at first drew them together,—those once sacred
features, that magical play of charms,—was deciduous, and a
prospective end, like the scaffolding by which the house was built ;
and the purification of the intellect and the heart, from year to year, is
the real marriage, foreseen and prepared from the first, and wholly
above their consciousness.   Looking at these aims, with which two
persons, a man and a woman, so variously and correlatively gifted, are
shut up in one house to spend in the nuptial society forty or fifty years,
I do not wonder at the emphasis with which the heart prophesies this
crisis from early infancy, at the profuse beauty with which the instincts
deck the nuptial bower, and nature and intellect and art emulate each
other in the gifts and melody they bring to the epithalamium.

Thus we are put in training for a love which knows not sex, nor
person, nor partiality, but which seeketh virtue and wisdom
everywhere, to the end of increasing virtue and wisdom.   We are by
nature observers, and thereby learners : that is our permanent state.
But we are often made to feel that our affections are but tents of a
night.   Though slowly and with pain, the objects of the affections
change, as the objects of thought do.   There are moment when the
affections rule and absorb the man, and make his happiness dependent
on a person or persons.   But in health the mind is presently seen again

—its overarching vault, bright with galaxies of immutable lights, and the warm loves and fears that swept over us as clues, must lose their finite character, and blend with God, to attain their own perfection. But we need not fear that we can lose any thing by the progress of the soul.   The soul may be trusted to the end.   That which is so beautiful and attractive in these relations, must be succeeded and supplanted only by what is more beautiful, and so on for ever.

FRIENDSHIP

Edited by A.D Hendry
Cover Art by A.D Hendry

We have a great deal more kindness than is ever spoken.   Maugre
all the selfishness that chills like east winds the world, the whole
human family is bathed with an element of love like a fine ether.   How
many persons we meet in houses, whom we scarcely speak to, whom
yet we honour, and who honour us !   How many we see in the street,
or sit with in church, whom, though silently, we warmly rejoice to be
with !   Read the language of these wandering eye-beams.   The heart
knoweth.

The effect of the indulgence of this human affection is a certain
cordial exhilaration.   In poetry and in common speech, the emotions
of benevolence and complacency which are felt towards others are
likened to the material effects of fire ; so swift, or much more swift,
more active, more cheering, are these fine inward irradiations.   From
the highest degree of passionate love, to the lowest degree of good
will, they make the sweetness of life.   Our intellectual and active
powers increase with our affection.   The scholar sits down to write,
and all his years of meditation do no furnish him with one good
thought or happy expression ; but it is necessary to write a letter to a
friend,— and forthwith troops of gentle thoughts invest themselves, on
every hand, with chosen words.   See, in any house where virtue and
self-respect abide, the palpitation which the approach of a stranger
causes.   A commended stranger is expected and announced, and an
uneasiness betwixt pleasure and pain invades all the hearts of a
household.   His arrival brings fear to the good hearts that would
welcome him.   The house is dusted, all things fly into their places, the
old coat is exchanged for the new, and they must get up a dinner if
they can.   Of a commended stranger, only the good report is told by
others, only the good and new is heard by us.   He stands to us for
humanity.   He is what we wish.   Having imagined and invested him,
we ask how we should stand related in conversation and action with
such a man, and are uneasy with fear.   The same idea exalts
conversation with him.   We talk better than we are wont.   We have the
nimblest fancy, a richer time.   For long hours we can continue a series
of sincere, grateful, rich communications, drawn from the oldest,

secretest experience, so that they who sit by, of our own kinsfolk and acquaintance, shall feel a lively surprise at our unusual powers.   But as soon as the stranger begins to intrude his partialities, his definitions, his effects, into the conversation, it is all over.   He has heard the first, the last and best, he will ever hear from us.   He is no stranger now. Vulgarity, ignorance, misapprehension, are old acquaintances.   Now when he comes, he may get the order, the dress, the dinner,—but the throbbing of the heart, and the communications of the soul, no more.

Pleasant are these jets of affection, which relume a young world for me again.   Delicious is a just and firm encounter of two in a thought, a feeling.   How beautiful, on their approach to this beating heart, the steps and the forms of the gifted and the true !   The moment we indulge our affections, the earth is metamorphosed : there is no winter, and no night : all tragedies, all ennuis vanish; all duties even ; nothing fills the proceeding eternity but the forms all radiant of beloved persons.   Let the soul be assured that somewhere in the universe it should rejoin its friend, and it would be content and cheerful alone for a thousand years.

I awoke this morning with devout thanksgiving for my friends, the old and the new.   Shall I not call God the Beautiful, who daily sheweth himself so to me in his gifts ?   I chide society, I embrace solitude, and yet I am not so ungrateful as not to see the wise, the lovely and the noble-minded, as from time to time they pass my gate. Who hears me, who understands me, becomes mine,—a possession for all time.   Nor is nature so poor, but she gives me this joy several times, and thus we weave social threads of our own, a new web of relations ; and, as many thoughts in succession substantiate themselves, we shall by and by stand in a new world of our own creation, and no longer strangers and pilgrims in a traditionary globe. My friends have come to me unsought.   The great God gave them to me.   By oldest right, by the divine affinity of virtue with itself, I find them, or rather not I, but the Deity in me and in them, both deride and cancel the thick walls of individual character, relation, age, sex and circumstance, at which he usually connives, and now many makes one. High thanks I owe you, excellent lovers, who carry out the world for me to new and noble depths, and enlarge the meaning of all my thoughts.   These are not stark and stiffened persons, but the new-born poetry of God,—poetry without stop—hymn, ode and epic, poetry still flowing, and not yet caked in dead books with annotations and grammar, but Apollo and the muses chanting still.   Will these two separate themselves from me again, or some of them ?   I know not, but I fear it not ; for my relation to them is so pure, that we hold by simple affinity, and the Genius of my life being thus social, the same affinity will exert its energy on whomsoever is as noble as these men and women, wherever I may be.

I confess to an extreme tenderness of nature on this point.   It is almost dangerous to me to " crush the sweet poison of misused wine" of the affections.   A new person is to me always a great event, and hinders me from sleep.   I have had such fine fancies lately about two or three persons, as have given me delicious hours ; but the joy ends in the day : it yields no fruit.   Thought is not born of it ; my action is very little modified.   I must feel pride in my friend's accomplishments, as if they were mine—wild, delicate, throbbing property in his virtues.   I feel as warmly when he is praised, as the lover when he hears applause of his engaged maiden.   We over-estimate the conscience of our friend.   His goodness seems better than our goodness, his nature finer, his temptations less.   Every thing that is his, his name, his form, his dress, books, and instruments, fancy enhances.   Our own thought sounds new and larger from his mouth.

Yet the systole and diastole of the heart are not without their analogy in the ebb and flow of love.   Friendship, like the immortality of the soul, is too good to be believed.   The lover, beholding his maiden, half knows that she is not verily that which he worships ; and in the golden hour of friendship, we are surprised with shades of suspicion and unbelief.   We doubt that we bestow on our hero the virtues in which he shines, and afterwards worship the form to which we have ascribed this divine inhabitation. In strictness, the soul does not respect men as it respects itself. In strict science, all persons underlie the same condition of an infinite remoteness. Shall we fear to cool our love by facing the fact, by mining for the metaphysical foundation of this Elysian temple ? Shall I not be as real as the things I see ? If I am, I shall not fear to know them for what they are. Their essence is not less beautiful than their appearance, though it needs finer organs for its apprehension. The root of the plant is not unsightly to science, though for chaplets and festoons we cut the stems short. And I must hazard the production of the bald fact amidst these pleasing reveries, though it should prove an Egyptian skull at our banquet. A man who stands united with his thought conceives magnificently of himself. He is conscious of a universal success, even though bought by uniform particular failures. No advantages, no powers, no gold or force can be any match for him. I cannot choose but rely on my own poverty more than on your wealth. I cannot make your conscious tantamount to mine. Only the star dazzles ; the planet has a faint, moon-like ray. I hear what you say of the admirable parts and tried temper of the party you praise, but I see well that for all his purple cloaks I shall not like him, unless he is at last a poor Greek like me. I cannot deny it, O friend, that the vast shadow of the Phenomenal includes thee also in its pied and painted immensity,— thee also, compared with whom all else is shadow. Thou art not Being, as Truth is, as Justice is, —thou art not my soul, but a picture and effigy of that. Thou hast come to me lately, and already thou art seizing thy hat and cloak. Is it not that the soul puts forth from friends, as the tree puts forth leaves, and presently, by the germination of new buds, extrudes the old leaf ? The law of nature is alteration forever more. Each electrical state superinduces the opposite. The soul environs itself with friends, that it may enter into a grander self-acquaintance or solitude ; and it goes alone for a season, that it may exalt its conversation or society. This method betrays itself along the whole history of our personal relations. Ever the instinct of affection revives the hope of union with our mates, and ever the returning sense of insulation recalls us from the chase. Thus every man passes his life

in the search after friendship ; and if he should record his true
sentiment, he might write a letter like this to each new candidate for
his love.

DEAR FRIEND,

If I was so sure of thee, sure of thy capacity, sure
to match my mood with thine, I should never think again of trifles, in
relation to thy comings and goings. I am not very wise ; my moods
are quite attainable : and I respect thy genius : it is to me as yet
unfathomed ; yet dare I not presume in thee a perfect intelligence of
me, and so thou art to me a delicious torment. Thine ever, or never.

Yet these uneasy pleasures and fine pains are for curiosity, and not
for life. They are not to be indulged. This is to weave cobweb, and
not cloth. Our friendships hurry to short and poor conclusions,
because we have made them a texture of wine and dreams, instead of
the tough fibre of the human heart. The laws of friendship are great,
austere, and eternal, of one web with the laws of nature and of morals.
But we have aimed at a swift and petty benefit, to such a sudden
sweetness. We snatch at the slowest fruit in the whole garden of God,
which many summers and many winters must ripen. We seek out
friend not sacredly, but with an adulterate passion, which would
appropriate him to ourselves. In vain. We are armed all over with
subtle antagonisms, which, as soon as we meet, begin to play, and
translate all poetry into stale prose. Almost all people descend to
meet. All association must be a compromise, and, what is worst, the
very flower and aroma of the flower of each of the beautiful natures
disappears as they approach each other. What a perpetual
disappointment is actual society, even of the virtuous and gifted ! After
interviews have been compassed with long foresight, we must be
tormented presently by baffled blows, by sudden unseasonable
apathies, by epilepsies of wit and of animal spirits, in the hey-day of
friendship and thought. Our faculties do not play us true, and both
parties are relieved by solitude. I ought to be equal to every relation.
It makes no difference how many friends I have, and what content I

can find in conversing with each, if there be one to whom I am not
equal. If I have shrunk unequal from one contest, instantly the joy I
find in all the rest becomes mean and cowardly. I should hate myself,
if then I made my other friends my asylum.

" The valiant warrior famoused for fight,

After a hundred victories, once foiled,

Is from the book of honour razed quite,

And all the rest forget for which he toiled."

Our impatience is thus sharply rebuked. Bashfulness and apathy
are a tough husk, in which delicate organisation is protected from
premature ripening. It would be lost, if it knew itself before any of
the best souls were yet ripe enough to know and own it. Respect the
Naturelangsamkeit which hardens the ruby in a million years, and
works in duration, in which Alps and Andes come and go as rainbows.
The good spirit of our life has no heaven which is the price of
rashness. Love, which is the essence of God, is not for levity, but for
total worth of man. Let us not have this childish luxury in our
regards, but the austerest worth ; let us approach our friend with an
audacious trust in the truth of his heart, in the breadth, impossible to be
overturned, of his foundations.

The attractions of this subject are not to be resisted ; and I leave,
for the time, all account of subordinate social benefit, to speak of that
select and sacred relation which is a kind of absolute, and which even
leaves the language of love auspicious and common, so much is this
purer, and nothing is so much divine.

I do not wish to treat friendships daintily, but with roughest courage.   When they are real, they are not glass threads or frost-work, but the solidest thing we know.   For now, after so many ages experience, what do we know of nature, or of ourselves ?   Not one step has man taken toward the solution of the problem of his destiny.   In one condemnation of folly stand the whole universe of men.   But the sweet sincerity of joy and peace, which I draw from this alliance with my brother's soul, is the nut itself whereof all nature and all thought is but the husk and shell.   Happy is the house that shelters a friend !   It might well be built, like a festal bower or arch, to entertain him a single day.   Happier, if he knows the solemnity of that relation, and honour its laws !   It is no idle band, no holiday engagement.   He who offers himself a candidate for that covenant comes up, like an Olympian, to the great games, where the firstborn of the world are competitors.   He proposes himself for contests where Time, Want, Danger, are in the lists, and he alone is victor who has truth enough in his constitution to preserve the delicacy of his beauty from the wear and tear of all these.   The gifts of fortune may be present or absent, but all the hap in that contest depends on intrinsic nobleness, and the contempt of trifles.   There are two elements that go to the composition of friendship, each so sovereign, that I can detect no superiority in either, no reason why either should be first named.   One is Truth.   A friend is a person with who I may be sincere.   Before him I may think aloud.   I am arrived at last in the presence of a man so real and equal, that I may drop even those undermost garments of dissimulation, courtesy and second thought, which men may never put off, and may deal with him with the simplicity and wholeness with which one chemical atom meets another.   Sincerity is the luxury allowed, like diadems and authority, only to the highest rank, *that* being permitted to speak truth, as having none above it to court or conform unto.   At the entrance of a second person, hypocrisy begins.   We parry and fend the approach of our fellow by many compliments, by gossip, by amusements, by affairs.   We cover up our thought from him in a hundred folds.   I knew a man who, under a certain religious frenzy, cast off this drapery, and, omitting all compliment and commonplace, spoke to the conscience he encountered, and that with great insight and beauty. At first he was resisted, and all men agreed he was mad. But persisting, as indeed he could not help doing, for some time in this course, he attained to the advantage of bringing every man of his acquaintance into true relations with him. No man would think of speaking falsely with him, or of putting him off with any chat of markets or reading-rooms. But every man was constrained by so much sincerity to face him, and what love of nature, what poetry, what symbol of truth he had, he did certainly shew him. But to most of us society shews not its face and eye, but its side and its back. To stand in true relations with men in a false age is worth a fit of insanity, is it not ? We can seldom go erect. Almost every man we meet requires some civility, requires to be humoured ;—he has some fame, some talent, some whim of religion or philanthropy in his head that is not to be questioned, and so spoils all conversation with him. But a friend is a sane man that exercises not my ingenuity, but me. My friend gives me entertainment without requiring me to stoop, or to lisp, or to mask myself. A friend, therefore, is a sort of paradox in nature. I who alone am, I see nothing in nature whose existence I can affirm with equal evidence to my own, behold now the semblance of my being in all its height, variety, and curiosity, reiterated in a foreign form ; so that a friend may well be reckoned the masterpiece of nature.

The other elements of friendship is Tenderness. We are holden to men by every sort of tie, by blood, by pride, by fear, by hope, by lucre, by lust, by hate, by admiration, by every circumstance and badge and trifle, but we can scarce believe that so much character can subsist in another as to draw us by love. Can another be so blessed, and we so pure, that we can offer him tenderness ? When a man becomes dear to me, I have touched the goal of fortune. I find very little written directly to the heart of this matter in books. And yet I have one text which I cannot choose but remember. My author says, " I offer myself faintly and bluntly to those whose I effectually am, and tender myself least to him to whom I am most devoted." I wish that friendship should have feet, as well as eyes and eloquence. It must plants itself on the ground, before it walks over the moon. I wish it to be a little a little of a citizen, before it is quite a cherub. We chide the citizen because he makes love a commodity. It is an exchange of gifts, of useful loans ; it is good neighbourhood ; it watches with the sick ; it holds the pall at the funeral ; and quite loses sight of the delicacies and nobility of the relation. But though we cannot find the God under this disguise of a sutler yet, on the other hand, we cannot forgive the poet, if he spins his thread too fine, and does not substantiate his romance by the municipal virtues of justice, punctuality, fidelity and pity. I hate the prostitution of the name of friendship to signify modish and world alliances. I much prefer the company of plough-boys and tin-pedlars to the silken and perfumed amity which only celebrates its day of encounter by a frivolous display, by rides in a curricle, and dinners at the best taverns. The end of friendship is a commerce the most strict and holy that can be joined ; more strict than any of which we have experience. It is for aid and comfort through all the relations and passages of life and death. It is for for serene days, and graceful gifts, and country rambles, but also for rough roads and hard fare, shipwreck, poverty, and persecution. It keeps company with the sallies of the wit and the trances of religion. We are to dignify to each other the daily needs and offices of man's life, and embellish it by courage, wisdom, and unity. It should never fall into something usual and settled, but should be alert and inventive, and add rhyme and reason to what was drudgery.

For perfect friendship it may be said to require natures so rare and costly, so well tempered each, and so happily adapted, a withal so circumstanced, (for even in that particular, a poet says, love demands that the parties be altogether paired,) that very seldom can its satisfaction be realised. It cannot subsist in its perfection, say some of those who are learned in this warm lore of the heart, betwixt more than two. I am not quite so strict in my terms, perhaps because I have never known so high a fellowship as others. I please my imagination more with a circle of godlike men and women variously related to each other, and between whom sits a lofty intelligence. But I find this law of *one to one* peremptory for conversation, which is the practice and consummation of friendship. Do not mix waters too much. The best mix as ill as good and bad. You shall have very useful and cheering discourse at several times with two several men ; but let all three of you come together, and you shall not have one new and hearty word. Two may talk and one may hear, but three cannot take part in a conversation of the most sincere and searching sort. In good company there is never such discourse between two, across the table, as takes place when you leave them alone. In good company, the individuals at once merge their egotism into a social soul exactly coextensive with the several consciousnesses there present. No partialities of friend to friend, no fondness of brother to sister, of wife to husband, are there pertinent, but quite otherwise. Only he may then speak who can sail on to his own. Now this convention, which good sense demands, destroys the high freedom of great conversation, which requires an absolute running of two souls into one. No two men but being left alone with each other enter into simpler relations. Yet it is affinity that determines *which* two shall converse. Unrelated men give little joy to each other ; will never suspect the latent powers of each. We talk sometimes of a great talent for conversation, as if it were a permanent property in some individuals. Conversation is an evanescent relation, —no more. A man is reputed to have thought an eloquence ; he cannot, for all that, say a word to his cousin or his uncle. They accuse his silence with has much significance of a dial in the shade. In the sun it will mark the hour. Among those who enjoy his thought, he will regain his tongue. Friendship requires that rare mean betwixt likeness and unlikeness, that piques each with the presence of power and of consent in the other party. Let me be alone to the end of the world, rather than that my friend should overstep by a word or a look in his real sympathy. I am equally baulked by antagonism and by compliance. Let him not cease an instant to be himself. The only joy I have in his being mine, is that the *not mine* is *mine.* It turns the stomach, it blots the daylight, where I looked for manly furtherance, or at least a manly resistance, to find a mush of

concession. Better be a nettle in the side of your friend than his echo.
The condition which high friendship demands is, ability to do without
it. To be capable of that high office requires great and sublime parts.
There must be very two, before there can be very one. Let it be an
alliance of two formidable natures, mutually beheld, mutually feared,
before yet they recognise the deep identity which beneath these
disparities unites them.

   He only is fit for this society who is magnanimous. He must be
so, to know its law. He must be one who is sure that greatness and
goodness are always economy. He must be one who is not sift to
intermeddle with his fortunes. Let him not dare to intermeddle with
this. Leave to the diamond its ages to grow, nor expect to accelerate
the briths of the eternal. Friendship demands a religious treatment.
We must not be wilful, we must not provide. We talk of choosing our
friends, but friends are self-elected. Reverence is a great part of it.
Treat your friend as a spectacle. Of course, if he be a man, he has
merits that are not yours, and that you cannot honour, if you must
needs hold him close to your person. Stand aside. Give those merits
room. Let them mount and expand. Be not so much his friend that
you can never know his peculiar energies ; like fond mammas who
shut up their boy in the house until he is almost grown a girl. Are you
the friend of your friend's buttons, or of his thought ? To a great heart
he will be a stranger in a thousand particulars, that he may come near
in the holiest ground. Leave it to girls and boys to regard a friend as
property, and to suck a short and all-confounding pleasure instead of
the pure nectar of God.

   Let us buy our entrance to this guild by a long probation. Why
should we desecrate noble and beautiful souls by intruding on them ?
Why insist on rash personal relations with your friend ? Why go to
his house, or know his mother and brother and sisters ? Why be
visited by him at your own ? Are these things material to our
covenant ? Leave this touching and clawing. Let him be to me a
spirit. A message, a thought, a sincerity, a glance from him, I want,

but not news, or pottage. I can get politics, and chat, and neighbourly conveniences, from cheaper companions. Should not the society of my friend be to me poetic, pure, universal, and great as nature itself ? Ought I to feel that our tie is profane in comparison to yonder bar of cloud that sleeps on the horizon, or that clump of waving grass that divides the brook ? Let us not vilify, but raise it to that standard. That great defying eye, that scornful beauty of his mien and action, do not pique yourself on reducing, but rather fortify and enhance. Worship his superiorities. Wish him not less by a thought, but hoard and tell them all. Guard him as thy great counterpart ; have a princedom to thy friend. Let him be to thee forever a sort of beautiful enemy, untameable, devoutly revered ; and not a trivial convenience, to be soon out-grown and cast aside. The hues of the opal, the light of the diamond, are not to be seen, if the eye is too near. To my friend I write a letter, and from him I receive a letter. That seems to you a little. Me it suffices. It is a spiritual gift worthy of him to give and of me to receive. It profanes nobody. In these warm lines the heart will trust itself, as it will not to the tongue, and pour out the property of a godlier existence that all the annals of heroism have yet made good.

Respect so far the holy laws of this fellowship as not to prejudice its perfect flower by your impatience for its opening. We must be our own, before we can be another's. There is at least this satisfaction in crime, according to the Latin proverb, you can speak to your accomplice on even terms.

Crimen, quos inquinant, æquat

To those whom we admire and love, at first we cannot. Yet the least defect of self-possession vitiates, in my judgement, the entire relation. There can never be deep peace between two spirits, never mutual respect, until in their dialogue, each stands for the whole world.

What is so great as friendship, let us carry with what grandeur of spirit we can. Let us be silent, —so we may hear the whisper of the gods. Let us not interfere. Who set you to cast about what you should say to the select souls, or to say any thing to such ?   No matter how ingenious, no matter how graceful and bland.   There are innumerable degrees of folly and wisdom ; and for you to say ought is to be frivolous.   Wait, and thy soul shall speak.   Wait until the necessary and everlasting overpowers you, until day and night avail themselves of your lips.   The only money of God is God.   He pays never with any thing less, or any thing else.   The only reward of virtue is virtue : the only way to have a friend is to be one.   Vain to hope to come nearer a man by getting into his house.   If unlike, his soul only flees the faster from you, and you shall catch never a true glance of his eye.   We see the noble afar off, and they repel us ; why should we intrude ?   Late—very late—we perceive that no arrangements, no introductions, no consuetudes, or habits of society, would be of any avail to establish us in such relations with them as we desire,—but solely the uprise of nature in us to the same degree it is in them : then we shall meet as water with water : and if we should not meet them then, we shall not want them, for we are already they.   In the last analysis, love is only the reflection of a man's own worthiness from other men.   Men have sometimes exchanged names with their friends, as if they would signify that in their friend each loved his own soul. The higher the style we demand of friendship, of course the less easy to establish it with flesh and blood.   We walk alone in the world. Friends such as we desire are dreams and fables.   But a sublime hope cheers ever the faithful heart, that elsewhere, in other regions of the universal power, souls are now acting, enduring, and daring, which can love us, and which we can love.   We may congratulate ourselves that the period of nonage, of follies, of blunders, and of shame, is passed in solitude, and when we are finished men, we shall grasp heroic hands in heroic hands.   Only be admonished by what you already see, not to strike leagues of friendship with cheap persons, where no friendship can be.   Our impatience betrays us into rash and foolish alliances, which no God attends.   By persisting in your path, though you forfeit the little, you gain the great.   You become pronounced.   You demonstrate yourself, so as to put yourself out of the reach of false-relations, and you draw to you the first-born of the world,—those rare pilgrims whereof only one or two wander in nature at once, and before whom the vulgar great shew as spectres and shadows merely.

It is foolish to be afraid of making our ties too spiritual, as if so we could lose any genuine love.   Whatever correction of our popular view we make from insight, nature will be sure to bear us out in, and though it seems to rob us of some joy, will repay us with a greater.   Let us feel, if we will, the absolute insulation of man.   We are sure that we have all in us.   We go to Europe, or we pursue persons, or we read books, in the instinctive faith that these will call it out and reveal us to ourselves.   Beggars all.   The persons are such as we ; the Europe, an old faded garment of dead persons ; the books, their ghosts.   Let us drop this idolatry.   Let us give over this mendicancy.   Let us even bid our dearest friends farewell, and defy them, saying, " Who are you? Unhand me : I will be dependent no more."   Ah ! seest thou not, O brother, that thus we part only to meet again on a higher platform, and only be more each other's, because we are more our own ?   A friend is Janus-faced : he looks to the past and the future.   He is the child of all my foregoing hours, the prophet of those to come.   He is the harbinger of a greater friend.   It is the property of the divine to be reproductive.

I do, then, with my friends as I do with my books.   I would have them where I can find them, but I seldom use them.   We must have society on our own terms, and admit or exclude it on the slightest cause.   I cannot afford to speak much with my friend.   If he is great, he makes me so great that I cannot descend to converse.   In the great days, presentiments hover before me, far before me in the firmament. I ought then to dedicate myself to them.   I go in that I may seize them, I go out that I may seize them.   I fear only that I may lose them receding into the sky in which now they are only a patch of brighter light.   Then, though I prize my friends, I cannot afford to talk with them and study their visions, lest I lose my own.   It would indeed give me a certain household joy to quit this lofty seeking, this spiritual astronomy, or search of stars, and come down to warm sympathies with you ; but then I know well I shall mourn always the vanishing of my mighty gods. It is true, next week I shall have languid times, when I can well afford to occupy myself with foreign objects ; then I shall regret the lost literature of your mind, and wish you were by my side again. But if you come, perhaps you will fill my mind only with new visions, not with yourself, but with lustres, and I shall not be able any more than now to converse with you. So I shall owe to my friends this evanescent intercourse. I will receive from them not what they have, but what they are. They shall give me that which properly they cannot give me, but which radiates from them. But they shall not hold me by any relations less subtle and pure. We will meet as though we met not, and part as though we parted not.

It has seemed to me lately more possible than I knew, to carry a friendship greatly, on one side, without due correspondence on the other. Why should I cumber myself with the poor fact that the receiver is not capacious? It never troubles the sun that some of his rays fall wide and vain into ungrateful space, and only a small part on the reflecting planet. Let your greatness educate the crude and cold companion. If he is unequal, he will presently pass away ; but thou art enlarged by thy own shining, and, no longer a mate for frogs and worms, dost soar and burn with the gods of the empyrean. It is thought a disgrace to love unrequited. But the great will see that true love cannot be unrequited. True love transcends instantly the unworthy object, and dwells and broods on the eternal ; and when the poor, interposed mask crumbles, it is not sad, but feels rid of so much earth, and feels its independency the surer. Yet these things may hardly be said without a sort of entireness, a total magnanimity and trust. It must not surmise or provide for infirmity. It treats object as a god, that it may deify both.

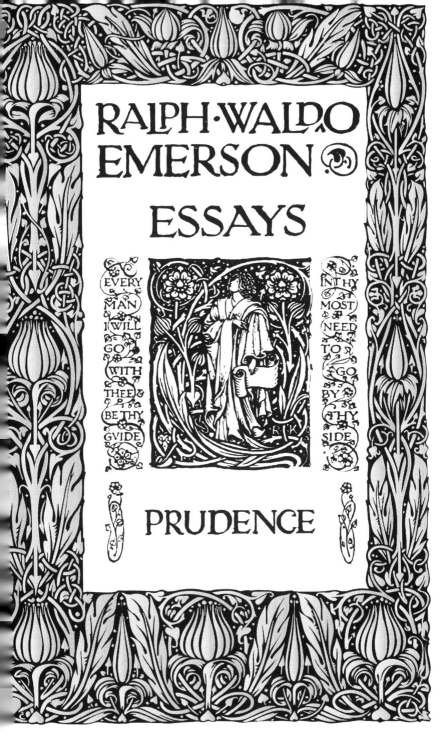

RALPH·WALDO
EMERSON

ESSAYS

EVERY MAN I WILL GO WITH THEE & BE THY GVIDE

IN THY MOST NEED TO GO BY THY SIDE

PRUDENCE

PRUDENCE

Edited by A.D Hendry
Cover Art by A.D Hendry

What right have I to write on Prudence, whereof I have little, and that of the negative sort ? My prudence consists in avoiding and going without, not in the inventing of means and methods, not in adroit steering, not in gentle repairing. I have no skill to make money spend well, no genius in my economy, and whoever sees my garden discovers that I must have some other garden. Yet I love facts, and hate lubricity and people without perception. Then I have the same title to write on prudence, that I have to write on poetry or holiness. We write from aspiration and antagonism, as well as from experience. We paint those qualities which we do not possess. The poet admires the man of energy and tactics ; the merchant breeds his son for the church or the bar : and where a man is not vain and egotistic, you shall find what he has not by his praise. Moreover it would be hardly honest in me not to balance these fine lyric words of Love and Friendship with words of coarser sound, and whilst my debt to my senses is real and constant, not to own it in passing.

Prudence is the virtue of the senses. It is the science of appearances. It is the outmost action of the inward life. It is God taking thought for oxen. It moves matter after the laws of matter. It is content to seek health of body by complying with physical conditions, and health of mind by the laws of the intellect.

The world of the senses is a world of shows ; it does not exist for itself, but has a symbolic character ; and a true prudence or law of shows recognises the co-presence of other laws, and knows that its own office is subaltern, knows that it is surface and not centre where it works. Prudence is false when detached. It is legitimate when it is the Natural History of the soul incarnate ; when it unfolds the beauty of laws within the narrow scope of the senses.

There are all degrees of proficiency in knowledge of the world. It is sufficient to our present purpose to indicate three. One class live to the utility of the symbol ; esteeming health and wealth a final good. Another class live above this mark, to the beauty of the symbol ; as the poet, and artist, and the naturalist, and man of science. A third class live above the beauty of the symbol, to the beauty of the thing signified ; these are wise men. The first class have common sense ; the second, taste ; and the third, spiritual perception. Once in a long time a man traverses the whole scale, and sees and enjoys the symbol solidly ; then also has a clear eye for it's beauty ; and lastly, whilst he pitches his tent on this sacred volcanic isle of nature, does not offer to build houses and barns thereon, reverencing the splendour of the God which he sees bursting through each chink and cranny.

The world is filled with proverbs and acts and winkings of a base prudence, which is a devotion to matter, as if we possessed no other faculties than the palate, the nose, the touch, the eye, and ear ; a prudence which adores the Rule of Three, which never subscribes, which gives never, which lends seldom, and asks but one question of any project —Will it bake bread ? This is a disease like a thickening of the skin until the vital organs are destroyed. But culture, revealing the high origin of the apparent world, and aiming at the perfection of the man as the end, degrades every thing else, as health and bodily life, into means. It sees prudence not to be a several faculty, but a name for wisdom and virtue conversing with the body and its wants. Cultivated men always feel and speak so, as if a great fortune, the achievement of a civil or social measure, great personal influence, a graceful and commanding address, had their value as proofs of the energy of the spirit. If a man lose his balance, and immerse himself in any trades or pleasures for their own sake, he may be a good wheel or pin, but he is not a cultivated man.

The spurious prudence, making the senses final, is the god of sots and cowards, and is the subject of all comedy. It is nature's joke, and therefore literature's. The true prudence limits the sensualism by admitting the knowledge of an internal and real world. This recognition once made,—the order of the world and the distribution of affairs and times being studied with the co-perception of their subordinate place, will reward any degree of attention. For, our existence thus apparently attached in nature to the sun and the returning moon and the periods which they mark,—so susceptible to climate and to country, so alive to social good and evil, so fond of splendour, and so tender to hunger and cold and debt,—reads all its primary lessons out of these books.

Prudence does not go behind nature, and ask, whence it is ? It takes the laws of the world, whereby man's being is conditioned, as they are, and keeps these laws, that it may enjoy their proper good. It respects space and time, climate, want, sleep, the law of polarity, and growth, and death. There revolve, to give bound and period to his being, on all sides, the sun and moon, the great formalists in the sky : here lies stubborn matter, and will not swerve from its chemical routine. Here is a painted globe, pierced and belted with natural laws, and fenced and distributed externally with civil partitions and properties which impose new restraints on the young inhabitant.

We eat of the bread which grows in the field. We live by the air which blows around us ; and we are poisoned by the air that is too cold or too hot, too dry or too wet. Time, which shews so vacant, indivisible, and divine in its coming, is slit and peddled into trifles and tatters. A door is to be painted, a lock to be repaired. I want wood, or oil, or meal, or salt ; the house smokes, or I have a headache ; then the tax ; and an affair to be transacted with a man without heart or brains ; and the stinging recollection of an injurious or very awkward word,— these eat up the hours. Do what we can, summer will have its flies. If we walk in the woods, we must feed mosquitoes. If we go a-fishing, we must expect a wet coat. Then climate is a great impediment to idle persons. We often resolve to give up the care of the weather, but still we regard the clouds and the rain.

We are instructed by these petty experiences which usurp the hours and years. The hard soil and four months of snow make the inhabitant of the northern temperate zone wiser and abler than his fellow who enjoys the fixed smile of the tropics. The islander may ramble all day at will. At night he may sleep on a mat under the moon ; and wherever a wild date-tree grows, nature has, without a prayer even,

spread a table for his morning meal.   The northerner is perforce a
house-holder.   He must brew, bake, and salt and preserve his food.
He must pile wood and coal.   But as it happens that not one stroke can
labour lay-to, without some new acquaintance with nature, and as
nature is inexhaustibly significant, the inhabitants of these climates
have always excelled the southerner in force.   Such is the value of
these matters, that a man who knows other things, can never know too
much of these.   Let him have accurate perceptions.   Let him, if he
have hands, handle ; if eyes, measure and discriminate ; let him accept
and hive every fact of chemistry, natural history, and economics ; the
more he has, the less he is willing to spare any one.   Time is always
bringing the occasions that disclose their value.   Some wisdom comes
out of every natural and innocent action.   The domestic man, who
loves no music so well as his kitchen clock, and the airs which the logs
sing to him as they burn on the hearth, has solaces which others never
dream of.   The application of means to ends ensures victory and the
songs of victory not less in a farm or a shop than in the tactics of party
or of war.   The good husband finds method as efficient in the packing
of fire-wood in a shed, or in the harvesting of fruits in the cellar, as in
the Peninsular campaigns or the files of the Department of State.   In
the rainy day he builds a work-bench, or gets his tool-box set in the
corner of the barn-chamber, and stored with nails, gimlet, pincers,
screwdriver, and chisel.   Herein he tastes an old joy of youth and
childhood, the cat-like love of garrets, presses, and corn-chambers, and
of the conveniences of long housekeeping.   His garden or his paltry-
yard,—very paltry places, it may be,—tell him many pleasant
anecdotes.   One might find argument for optimism in the abundant
flow of this saccharine element of pleasure in every suburb and
extremity of the good world.   Let a man keep the law,—any law,—and
his way will be strewn with satisfactions.   There is more difference in
the quality of our pleasures than in the amount.

On the other hand, nature punishes any neglect of prudence.   If
you think the senses final, obey their law.   If you believe in the soul,
do not clutch at sensual sweetness before it is ripe on the slow tree of

cause and effect.   It is vinegar to the eyes, to deal with men of loose
and imperfect perception.   Dr. Johnson is reported to have said, " If
the child says he looked out of this window, when he looked out of
that,—whip him."   Our American character is marked by a more than
average delight in accurate perception, which is shewn by the currency
of the by-word, " No mistake."   But the discomfort of unpunctuality,
of confusion of thought about facts, of inattention to the wants of to-
morrow, is of no nation.   The beautiful laws of time and space once
dislocated by our inaptitude, are holes and dens.   If the hive be
disturbed by rash and stupid hands, instead of honey it will yield us
bees.   Our words and actions to be fair must be timely.   A gay and
pleasant sound is the whetting of the scythe in the mornings of June ;
yet what is more lonesome and sad than the sound of of a whetstone or
mower's rifle, when it is too late in the season to make hay ? Scatter-
brained and " afternoon men " spoil much more than their own affair,
in spoiling the temper of those who deal with them.   I have seen a
criticism on some paintings, of which I am reminded when I see the
shiftless and unhappy men who are not true to their senses.   The last
Grand Duke of Weimar, a man of superior understanding, said ; " I
have sometimes remarked in the presence of great works of art, and
just now especially, in Dresden, how much a certain property
contributes to the effect which gives life to the figures, and to the life
an irresistible truth.   This property is the hitting, in all the figures we
draw, the right centre of gravity.   I mean, the placing the figures firm
upon their feet, making the hands grasp, and fastening the eyes on the
spot where they should look.   Even lifeless figures, as vessels and
stools, —let them be drawn ever so correctly,— lose all effect so soon
as they lack the resting upon their centre of gravity, and have a certain
swimming and oscillating appearance.   The Raphael, in the Dresden
gallery, (the only greatly affecting picture which I have seen), is the
quietist and most passionless piece you can imagine ; a couple of
saints who worship the Virgin and Child.   Nevertheless it awakes a
deeper impression than the contortions of ten crucified martyrs.   For,
beside all the resistless beauty of form, it possesses in the highest
degree the property of the perpendicularity of all the figures."—This

perpendicularity we demand of all the figures in this picture of life. Let them stand on their feet, and not float and swing. Let us know where to find them. Let them discriminate between what they remember, and what they dreamed. Let them call a spade a spade. Let them give us facts, and honour their own senses with trust.

But what man shall dare tax another with imprudence ? Who is prudent ? The men we call greatest are least in this kingdom. There is a certain fatal dislocation in our relation to nature, distorting all our modes of living, and making every law our enemy, which seems at last to have aroused all the wit and virtue in the world to ponder the question of Reform. We must call the highest prudence to counsel, and ask why health and beauty and genius should now be the exception, rather than the rule of human nature ? We do not know the properties of plants and animals, and the laws of nature, through our sympathy with the same ; but this remains the dream of poets. Poetry and prudence should be coincident. Poets should be lawgivers ; that is, the boldest lyric inspiration should not chide and insult, but should announce and lead the civil code and the day's work. But now the two things seem irreconcilably parted. We have violated law upon law, until we stand amidst ruins ; and when by chance we espy a coincidence between reason and the phenomena, we are surprised. Beauty should be the dowry of every man and woman, as invariably as sensation ; but it is rare. Health or sound organisation should be universal. Genius should be the child of genius, and every child should be inspired ; but now it is not to be predicted of any child, and nowhere is it pure. We call partial half-lights, by courtesy, genius ; talent which converts itself to money, talent which glitters to-day, that it may dine and sleep well to-morrow ; and society is officered by *men of parts* as they are properly called, and not by divine men. These use their gifts to refine luxury, not to abolish it. Genius is always ascetic, and piety and love. Appetite shews to the finer souls as a disease, and they find beauty in rites and bounds that resist it.

We have found out fine names to cover our sensuality withal, but no gifts can raise intemperance. The man of talent affects to call his transgressions of the laws of the senses trivial, and to count them nothing considered with his devotion to his art. His art rebukes him. That never taught him lewdness, nor the love of wine, nor the wish to reap where he had not sowed. His art is less for every deduction from his holiness, and less for every defect of common sense. On him who scorned the world, as he said, the scorned world wreaks its revenge. He that despiseth small things will perish by little and little. Goethe's Tasso is very likely to be a pretty fair historical portrait, and that is true tragedy. It does not seem to me so genuine grief when some tyrannous Richard III. oppresses and slays a score of innocent persons, as when Antonio and Tasso, both apparently right, wrong each other. One living after the maxims of this world, and consistent and true to them ; the other fired with all divine sentiments, yet grasping also at the pleasures of sense, without submitting to their law. That is a grief we all feel, a know we cannot untie. Tasso's is no infrequent case in modern biography. A man of genius, of an ardent temperament, reckless of physical laws, self-indulgent, becomes presently unfortunate, querulous, a " discomfortable cousin," a thorn to himself and to others.

The scholar shames us by his bifold life. Whilst something higher than prudence is active, he is admirable ; when common sense is wanted, he is an incumbrance. Yesterday radiant with the light of an ideal world, in which he lives, the first of men, and now pressed by wants and by sickness, for which he must thank himself, none is so poor to do him reverence. He resembles the opium-eaters, whom travellers describe as frequenting the bazars of Constantinople, who skulk about all day, the most pitiful drivelers, yellow, emaciated, ragged, and sneaking : then, at evening, when the bazaars are open, they slink to the opium-shop, swallow their morsel, and become tranquil, glorious, and great. And who has not yet seen the tragedy of imprudent genius, struggling for years with paltry pecuniary difficulties, at last sinking, chilled, exhausted, and fruitless, like a giant slaughtered by pins ?

Is it not better that a man should accept the first pains and mortifications of this sort, which nature is not slack in sending him, as hints that he must expect no other good than the fruit of his own labour and self-denial ?   Health, bread, climate, social position, have their importance, and he will give them their due.   Let him esteem Nature a perpetual counsellor, and her perfections the exact measure of our deviation.   Let him make the night night, and the day day.   Let him control the habit of expense.   Let him see that as much wisdom may be expended on a private economy as on an empire, and as much wisdom may be drawn from it.   The laws of the world are written out for him on every piece of money in his hand.   There is nothing he will not be better for knowing, were it only the wisdom of Poor Richard ; or the State-street prudence of buying by the acre, to sell by the foot ; or the thrift of the agriculturist, to stick a tree between whiles, because it will grow whilst he sleeps ; or the prudence which consists in husbanding little strokes of the tool, little portions of time, particles of stock, and small gains.   The eye of prudence may never shut.   Iron, if kept at the ironmonger's, will rust.   Beer, if not brewed in the right state of the atmosphere, will sour.   Timber of ships will rot at sea, or, if laid up high and dry, will strain, warp, and dry-rot.   Money, if kept by us, yields no rent, and is liable to loss ; if invested, is liable to depreciation of the particular kind of stock.   Strike, says the smith ; the iron is white.   Keep the rake, says the haymaker, as nigh the scythe as you can, and the cart as nigh the rake.   Our Yankee trade is reputed to be very much on the extreme of this prudence.   It saves itself by its activity.   It takes bank notes—good, bad, clean, ragged, and saves itself by the speed with which it passes them off.   Iron cannot rust, nor beer sour, nor timber rot, nor calicoes go out of fashion, nor money-stocks depreciate, in the few swift moments which the Yankee suffers any one of them to remain in his possession.   In skating over thin ice, our safety is in our speed.

Let him learn a prudence of a higher strain.   Let him learn that everything in nature, even motes and feathers, go by law and not by luck, and that what he sows, he reaps.   By diligence and self-command, let him put the bread he eats at his own disposal, and not at that of others, that he may not stand in bitter and false relations to other men ; for the best good of wealth is freedom.   Let him practice the minor virtues.   How much of human life is lost in waiting !   Let him not makes his fellow-creatures wait.   How many words and promises are promises of conversation !   Let his be words of fate. When he sees a folded and sealed scrap of paper float round the globe in a pine ship, and come safe to the eye for which it was written, amidst a swarming population, let him likewise feel the admonition to integrate his being across all these distracting forces, and keep a slender human word among the storms, distances, and accidents that drive us hither and thither, and, by persistency, make the paltry force of one man reappear to redeem its pledge, after months and years, in the most distant climates.

We must not try to write the laws of any one virtue, looking at that only.   Human nature loves no contradictions, but is symmetrical.   The prudence which secures an outward well-being is not to be studied by one set of men, whilst heroism and holiness are studied by another, but they are reconcilable.   Prudence concerns the present time, persons, property, and existing forms.   But as every fact hath its roots in the soul, and if the soul were changed, would cease to be, or would become some other thing, therefore the proper administration of outward things will always rest on a just apprehension of their cause and origin ; that is, the good man will be the wise man, and the single-hearted the politic man.   Every violation of truth is not only a sort of suicide in the liar, but is a stab at the health of human society.   On the most profitable lie the course of events presently lays a destructive tax ; whilst frankness proves to be the best tactics, for it invites frankness, puts the parties on a consistent footing, and makes their business a friendship.   Trust men, and they will be true to you ; treat them greatly, and they will shew themselves great, though make an exception in your favour to all their rules of trade.

So, in regard to disagreeable and formidable things, prudence does not consist in evasion, or in a flight, but in courage. He who wishes to walk in the most peaceful parts of life with any serenity must screw himself up to a resolution. Let him front the object of his worst apprehension, and his stoutness will commonly make his fear groundless. The Latin proverb says, that " in battles the eye is first overcome." The eye is daunted, and greatly exaggerates the perils of the hour. Entire self-possession may make a battle very little more dangerous to life than a match at foils or at foot-ball. Examples are cited by soldiers, of men who have seen the cannon pointed, and the fire given to it, and who has stepped aside from the path of the ball. The terrors of the storm are chiefly confined to the parlour and the cabin. The drover, the sailor, buffets it all day, and his health renews itself at as vigorous a pulse under the sleet, as under the sun of June.

In the occurrence of unpleasant things among neighbours fear comes readily to heart, and magnifies the consequence of the other party ; but it is a bad counsellor. Every man is actually weak, and apparently strong. To himself, he seems weak ; to others, formidable. You are afraid of Grim ; but Grim also is afraid of you. You are solicitous of the good will of the meanest person, uneasy at his ill will. But the sturdiest offender of your peace and of the neighbourhood, if you rip up *his* claims, is as thin and timid as any ; and the peace of society is often kept, because, as children say, one is afraid, and the other dares not. Far off, men swell, bully, and threaten ; bring them hand to hand and they are feeble folk.

It is a proverb, that " courtesy costs nothing " ; but calculation might come to value love for its profit. Love is fabled to be blind ; but kindness is necessary to perception ; love is not a hood, but an eye-water. If you meet a sectary, or a hostile partisan, never recognise the dividing lines ; but meet on what common ground remains, —if only that the sun shines, and the rain rains for both, —the area will widen

very fast, and ere you know it, the boundary mountains, on which the
eye had fastened, have melted into air.   If he set out to contend, almost
St. Paul will lie, almost St. John will hate.   What low, poor, paltry,
hypocritical people, an argument on religion will make of the pure and
chosen souls !   Shuffle they will, and crow, crook, and hide, feign to
confess here, only that they may brag and conquer there, and not a
thought has enriched either party, and not an emotion of bravery,
honesty, or hope.   So neither should you put yourself in a false
position to your contemporaries, by indulging in a view of hostility
and bitterness.   Though your views are in a straight antagonism to
theirs, assume an identity of sentiment, assume that you are saying
precisely that which all think, and in the flow of wit and love roll out
your paradoxes in solid column, with no the infirmity of a doubt.   So
at least shall you get an adequate deliverance.   The natural motions of
the soul are so much better than the voluntary ones, that you will never
do yourself justice in dispute.   The thought is not then taken hold of
by the right handle, does not shew itself proportioned, and in its true
bearings, but bears extorted, hoarse, and half witness.   But assume a
consent, and it shall presently be granted, since really, and underneath
all their external diversities, all men are of one heart and mind.

Wisdom will never let us stand with any man or men on an
unfriendly footing.   We refuse sympathy and intimacy with people, as
if we waited for some better sympathy and intimacy to come.   But
Whence and when ?   To-morrow will be like to-day.   Our friends and
fellow workers die off from us.   Scarcely can we say, we see new
men, new women approaching us.   We are too old to regard fashion,
too old to expect patronage of any greater or more powerful.   Let us
suck the sweetness of those affections and consuetudes that grow near
us.   These old shoes are easy to the feet.   Undoubtedly, we can easily
pick faults in our company, can easily whisper names prouder, and that
tickle the fancy more.   Every man's imagination hath its friends ; and
pleasant would life be with such companions.   But if you cannot have
them on good mutual terms, you cannot have them.   If not the Deity,

but our ambition hews and shapes the new relations, their virtue escapes, as strawberries lose their flavour in garden-beds.

Thus truth, frankness, courage, love, humility, and all virtues, range themselves on the side of prudence, or the art of securing a present well-being.   I do not know if all matter will be found to be made of one element, as oxygen or hydrogen, at last ; but the world of manners and actions is wrought of one stuff, and being where we will, we are pretty sure in a short space to be mumbling our ten commandments.

RALPH·WALDO EMERSON

ESSAYS

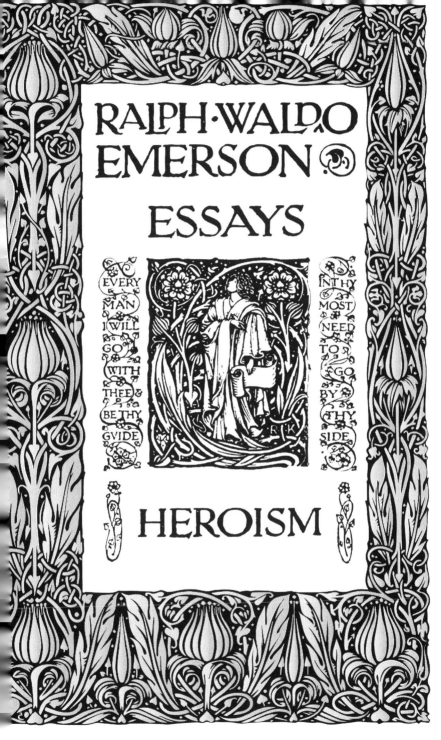

EVERY MAN I WILL GO WITH THEE & BE THY GVIDE

IN THY MOST NEED TO GO BY THY SIDE

HEROISM

HEROISM

" Paradise is under the shadow of swords."

Mahamet

Edited by A.D Hendry
Cover Art by A.D Hendry

In the elder English dramatists, and mainly in the plays of
Beaumont and Fletcher, there's a constant recognition of gentility, as if
a noble behaviour were as easily marked in the society of their age, as
colour is in our American population.   When any Rodrigo, Pedro, or
Valerio enters, though he be a stranger, the duke or governor exclaims,
This is a gentleman, —and proffers civilities without end ; but all the
rest are slug and refuse.   In harmony with this delight in personal
advantages, there is in their plays a certain heroic cast of character and
dialogue, —as in Bonduca, Sophocles, the Mad Lover, the Double
Marriage, —wherein the speaker is so earnest and cordial, and on such
deep grounds of character, that the dialogue, on the slightest additional
incident in the plot, rises naturally into poetry.   Among many texts,
take the following.   The Roman Martius has conquered Athens, —all
but the invincible spirits of Sophocles the duke of Athens, and Dorigen
his wife.   The beauty of the latter inflames Martius, and he seeks to
save her husband ; but Sophocles will not ask his life, although assured
that a word will save him, and the execution of both proceeds.

" *Valerius.*   Bid thy wife farewell

Soph.   No, I will take no leave.   My Dorigen,

Yonder above, 'bout Ariadne's crown,

My spirit shall hover for thee.   Prithee, haste.

Dor.   Stay, Sophocles, —with this tie up my sight ;

Let not soft nature so transformed be,

And lose her gentler-sexed humanity,

To make me see my lord bleed.   So, 'tis well ;

Never one object underneath the sun

Will I behold before my Sophocles.

Farewell ; now teach the Romans how to die.

    Mar.   Dost know what 'tis to die ?

    Soph.   Thou dost not, Martius,
And therefore not what 'tis to live.   To die
Is to begin to live ; it is to end
An old, stale, weary work, and to commence
A newer and a better ; tis to leave
Deceitful knaves for the society
of gods and goodness.   Thou thyself must part
At last from all thy garlands, pleasures, triumphs,
And prove thy fortitude what then 'twill do.

    Val.   But art not grieved or vexed to leave thy life thus ?

    Soph.   Why should I grieve or vex for being sent
To them I ever loved best ?   Now I'll kneel
But with my back toward thee ; 'tis the last duty
This trunk can do the gods.

    Mar.   Strike, strike, Valerius,
Or Martius' heart will leap out at his mouth :
This is a man, a woman !   Kiss thy lord,
And live with all the freedom you were wont.

O love ! thou doubly hast afflicted me
With virtue and with beauty.   Treacherous heart,
My hand shall cast thee quick into my urn,
Ere thou transgress this knot of piety.

    Val.   What ails my brother?

    Soph.   Martius, O Martius,
thou now hast found a way to conquer me.

    Dor.   O star of Rome ! what gratitude can speak
Fit words to follow such a deed as this?

    Mar.   This admirable duke, Valerius,
With his disdain of fortune and of death,
Captivated himself, has captivated me,
And though my arm hath ta'en his body here,
His soul hath subjugated Martius' soul.
By Romulus, he is all soul, I think ;
He hath no flesh, and spirit cannot be gyved.
Then we have vanquished nothing ; he is free,
And Martius walks now in captivity."

    I do not readily remember any poem, play, sermon, novel, or
oration, that our press vents in the last few years, which goes to the

same tune.   We have a great many flutes and flageolets, but not often
the sound of any fife.   Yet Wordsworth's Laodamia, and the ode of
" Dion," and some sonnets, have a certain noble music ; and Scott will
sometimes draw a stroke like the portrait of Lord Evandale, given by
Balfour or Burley.   Thomas Carlyle, with his natural taste for what is
manly and daring in character, has suffered no heroic trait in his
favourites to drop from his biographical and historical pictures.
Earlier, Robert Burns has given us a song or two.   In the Harlan
Miscellanies there is an account of the battle of Luton, which deserves
to be read.   And Simon Ockley's History of the Saracens recounts the
prodigies of individual valour with admiration, all the more evident on
the part of the narrator, that he seems to think that his place in
Christian Oxford requires of him some proper protestations of
abhorrence.   But if we explore the literature of Heroism, we shall
quickly come to Plutarch, who is its doctor and historian.   To him we
owe the Brasidas, the Dion, the Epaminondas, the Scipio of old ; and I
must think we are more deeply indebted to him than to all the ancient
writers.   Each of his " Lives" is a refutation to the despondency and
cowardice of our religious and political theorists.   A wild courage, a
stoicism not of the schools, but of the blood, shines in every anecdote,
and has given that book its immense fame.

We need books of this tart cathartic virtue, more than books of
political science or of private economy.   Life is a festal only to the
wise.   Seen from the nook and chimney-side of prudence, it wears a
ragged and dangerous front.   The violations of the laws of nature by
our predecessors and our contemporaries are punished in us also.   The
disease and deformity around us certify the infraction of natural,
intellectual, and moral laws, and often violation on violation to breed
such compound misery.   A lock-jaw, that bends a man's head back to
his heels ; hydrophobia, that makes him bark at his wife and babes ;
insanity, that makes him eat grass ; war, plague, cholera, famine, —
indicate a certain ferocity in nature, which, as it had its inlet by human
crime, must have its outlet by human suffering.   Unhappily, almost no
man exists who has not in his own person become, to some amount, a

stockholder in the sin, and so made himself liable to a share in the expiation.

Our culture, therefore, must not omit the arming of the man. Let him hear in season, that he is born into the state of war, and that the commonwealth and his own well-being require that he should not go dancing in the weeds of peace ; but warned, self-collected, and neither defying nor dreading the thunder, let him take both reputation and life in his hand, and with perfect urbanity dare the gibbet and the mob by the absolute truth of his speech and the rectitude of his behaviour.

Towards all this external evil the man within the breast assumes a warlike attitude, and affirms his ability to cope single-handed with the infinite army of enemies. To this military attitude of the soul we give the name of Heroism. Its rudest form is the contempt for safety and ease, which makes the attractiveness of war. It is a self-trust which slights the restraints of prudence, in the plenitude of its energy and power to repair the harms it may suffer. The hero is a mind of such balance that no disturbances can shake his will ; but pleasantly, and as it were merrily, he advances to his own music, alike in frightful alarms and in the tipsy mirth of universal dissoluteness. There is somewhat not philosophical in heroism ; there is somewhat not holy in it ; it seems not to know that other souls are of one texture with it ; it hath pride ; it is the extreme of individual nature. Nevertheless we must profoundly revere it. There is somewhat in great actions, which does not allow us to go behind them. Heroism feels and never reasons, and therefore is always right ; and although different breeding, different religion, and greater intellectual activity, would have modified or even reversed the particular action, yet for the hero, that thing he does is the highest deed, and is not open to the censure of philosophers or divines. It is the avowal of the unschooled man, that he finds a quality in him that is negligent of expense, of health, of life, of danger, of hatred, of reproach, and that he knows that his will is higher and more excellent than all actual and possible antagonists.

Heroism works in contradiction to the voice of mankind, and in contradiction, for a time, to the voice of the great and the good. Heroism is an obedience to a secret impulse of an individual's character. Now to no other man can its wisdom appear as it does to him, for every man must be supposed to see a little farther on his own proper path than any one else. Therefore, just and wise men take umbrage at his act, until after some little time be past ; then they see it to be in unison with their acts. All prudent men see that the action is clean contrary to a sensual prosperity ; for every heroic act measures itself by its contempt of some external good. But it finds its own success at last, and then the prudent also extol.

Self-trust is the essence of Heroism. It is the state of the soul at war ; and its ultimate objects are the last defiance of falsehood and wrong, and the power to bear all that can be inflicted by evil agents. It speaks the truth, and it is just. It is generous, hospitable, temperate, scornful of petty calculations, and scornful of being scorned. It persists ; it is of an undaunted boldness, and of a fortitude not to be wearied out. Its jest is the littleness of common life. That false prudence which dotes on health and wealth is the foil, the butt and merriment of heroism. Heroism, like Plotinus, is almost ashamed of its body. What shall it say, then, to the sugar-plums and cats-cradles, to the toilet, compliments, quarrels, cards, and custard, which rack the wit of all human society ? What joys has kind nature provided for us dear creatures ! There seems to be no interval between greatness and meanness. When the spirit is not master of the world, then is it its dupe. Yet the little man takes the great hoax so innocently, works in it so headlong and believing, is born red, and dies gray, arranging his toilet, attending on his own health, laying traps for sweet food and strong wine, setting his heart on a horse or a rifle, made happy with a little gossip or a little praise, that the great soul cannot choose but laugh at such earnest nonsense. " Indeed, these humble considerations make me out of love with greatness. What a disgrace is to me to take note how many pairs of silk stockings thou hast, namely, these and those that were the peach-coloured ones ; or to bear inventory of thy shirts, as one for superfluity, and one other for use ! ''

Citizens, thinking after the laws of arithmetic, consider the inconvenience of receiving strangers at their fireside, reckon narrowly the loss of time and the unusual display ; the soul of a better quality thrusts back the unseasonable economy into the vaults of life, and says, I will obey the God, and the sacrifice and the fire he will provide. Ibn Haukal, the Arabian geographer, describes a heroic extreme in the hospitality of Sogd, in Bukharia. " When I was in Sogd, I saw a great building, like a palace, the gates of which were open and fixed back to the wall with large nails. I asked the reason, and was told that the house has not been shut night or day, for a hundred years. Strangers may present themselves at any hour, and in whatever number ; the master has amply provided for the reception of the men and their animals, and is never happier when they tarry for some time. Nothing of the kind have I seen in any other country." The magnanimous know very well, that they who give time, or money, or shelter to the stranger—so it be done for love, and not for ostentation—do as it were put God under obligation to them, so perfect are the compensations of the universe. In some way, the time they seem to lose is redeemed, and the pains they seem to take remunerate themselves. These men fan the flame of human love, and raise the standard of civil virtue among mankind. But hospitality must be for service, and not for show, or it pulls down the host. The brave soul rates itself too high to value itself by the splendour of its table and draperies. It gives what it hath, and all it hath ; but its own majesty can lend a better grace to bannocks and fair water than belong to city feasts.

The temperance of the hero proceeds from the same wish to do no dishonour to the worthiness he has. But he loves it for its elegancy, not for its austerity. It seems not worth his while to be solemn, and denounce with bitterness flesh-eating or wine-drinking, the use of tobacco, or opium, or tea, or silk, or gold. A great man scarcely knows how he dines, how he dresses ; but, without railing or precision, his living is natural and poetic.   John Eliot, the Indian Apostle, drank water, and said of wine, " It is a noble, generous liquor, and we should be humbly thankful for it ; but, as I remember, water was made before it."   Better still is the temperance of king David, who poured out on the ground unto the Lord the water which three of his warriors had brought him to drink at the peril of their lives.

It is told of Brutus, that when he fell on his sword, after the battle of Philippi, he quoted a line of Euripides, " O virtue, I have followed thee through life, and I find thee at last but a shade."   I doubt not the hero is slandered by this report.   The heroic soul does not sell its justice and nobleness.   It does not ask to dine nicely and to sleep warm.   The essence of greatness is the perception that virtue is enough.   Poverty is its ornament.   Plenty it does not need, and can very well abide its loss.

But that which takes my fancy most, in the heroic class, is the good humour and hilarity which they exhibit.   It is a height to which common duty can very well attain, to suffer and to dare with solemnity.   But these rare souls set opinion, success, and life, at so cheap a rate, that they will not soothe their enemies by petitions, or the show of sorrow, but wear their own habitual greatness.   Scipio, charged with peculation, refuses to do himself so great a disgrace as to wait for justification, though he had the scroll of his accounts in his hands, but tears it to pieces before the tribunes.   Socrates' condemnation of himself to be maintained in all honour in the Prytaneum during his life, and Sir Thomas More's playfulness at the scaffold, are of the same strain. In Beaumont and Fletcher's " Sea Voyage," Juletta tells the stout captain and his company,

"*Jul.*   Why, slaves, 'tis in our power to hang ye.

Master.   Very likely ; 'tis in our powers then, to be hanged, and scorn ye."

These replies are sound and whole. Sport is the bloom and glow of a perfect health. The great will not condescend to take anything seriously ; all must be as gay as the song of a canary, though it were the building of cities, or the eradication of old and foolish churches and nations, which have cumbered the earth long thousands of years. Simple hearts put all the history and customs of this world behind them, and play their own play in innocent defiance of the Blue-Laws of the world ; and such would appear, could we see the human race assembled in vision, like little children frolicking together ; though, to the eyes of mankind at large, they wear a stately and solemn garb of works and influences.

The interest these fine stories have for us, the power of a romance over the boy who grasps the forbidden book under his bench at school, our delight in the hero, is the main fact to our purpose. All these great and transcendent properties are ours. If we dilate in beholding the Greek energy, the Roman pride, it is that we are already domesticating the same sentiment. Let us find room for this great guest in our small houses. The first step of worthiness will be to disabuse us of our superstitious associations with places and times, with number and size. Why should these words, Athenian, Roman, Asia, and England, so tingle in the ear ? Let us feel that where the heart is, there the muses, there the gods sojourn, and not in any geography of fame. Massachusetts, Connecticut River, and Boston Bay, you think paltry places, and the ear loves names of foreign and classic topography. But here we are ;—that is a great fact, and, if we tarry a little, we may come to learn that here is best. See to it, only that thyself is here ;— and art and nature, hope and dread, friends, angels, and the Supreme Being, shall not be best from the chamber where thou sittest. Epaminondas, brave and affectionate, does not seem to us to need Olympus to die upon, nor the Syrian sunshine. He lies very well where he is. The Jerseys were handsome ground enough for Washington to tread, and London streets for the feet of Milton. A great man illustrates his place, makes his climate genial in the imagination of men, and its air the beloved element of all delicate spirits. That country is fairest which is inhabited by the noblest minds. The pictures which fill the imagination in reading the actions of Pericles, Xenophon, Columbus, Bayard, Sidney, Hampden, teach us how needlessly mean our life is ; that we, by the depth of our living, should deck it with more than regal or national splendour, and act on principles that should interest man and nature in the length of our days.

We have seen or heard of many extraordinary young men who never ripened, or whose performance in actual life was not extraordinary. When we see their air and mien, when we hear them speak of society, of books, of religion, we admire their superiority, they seem to throw contempt on the whole state of the world ; theirs is the tone of a youthful giant, who is sent to work revolutions. But they enter an active profession, and the forming Colossus shrinks to the common size of man. The magic they used was the ideal tendencies, which always make the Actual ridiculous ; but the tough world had its revenge the moment they put their horses of the sun to plough in its furrow. They found no example and no companion, and their heart fainted. What then ? The lesson they gave in their first aspirations is yet true ; and a better valour and a purer truth shall one day execute their will, and put the world to shame. Or why should a woman liken herself to any historical woman, and think, because Sappho, or Sévigné, or De Staël, or the cloistered souls who have had genius and cultivation, do not satisfy the imagination and the serene Themis, none can,—certainly not she ? Why not ? She has a new and unattempted problem to solve, perchance that of the happiest nature that ever bloomed. Let the maiden with erect soul walk serenely on her way, accept the hint of each new experience, try, in turn, all the gifts God offers her, that she may learn the power and the charm that, like a new dawn radiating out of the deep of space, her new-born being is. The fair girl, who repels interference by a decided and proud choice of influences, so careless of pleasing, so wilful and lofty, inspires every beholder with somewhat of her own nobleness. The silent heart encourages her ; O friend, never strike sail to a fear. Come into port

greatly, or sail with God the seas.   Not in vain you live, for every
passing eye is cheered and refined by the vision.

The characteristic of a genuine heroism is its persistency.   All men
have wandering impulses, fits and starts of generosity.   But when you
have resolved to be great, abide by yourself, and do not weakly try to
reconcile yourself with the world.   The heroic cannot be the common,
nor the common the heroic.   Yet we have the weakness to expect the
sympathy of people in those actions whose excellence is, that they
outrun sympathy, and appeal to a tardy justice.   If you would serve
your brother, because it is fit for you to serve him, do not take back
your words when you find that prudent people do not commend you.
Be true to your own act, and congratulate yourself if you have done
something strange and extravagant, and broken the monotony of a
decorous age.   It was a high council that I once heard given to a young
person, " Always do what you are afraid to do."   A simple manly
character need never make an apology, but should regard its past
action with the calmness of Phocion, when he admitted that the event
of the battle was happy, yet did not regret his dissuasion from the
battle.

There is no weakness or exposure for which we cannot find
consolation in the thought,—this is a part of my constitution, part of
my relation and office to my fellow creature.   Has nature covenanted
with me that I should never appear to disadvantage, never make a
ridiculous figure ?   Let us be generous of our dignity, as well as our
money.   Greatness once and forever has done with opinion.   We tell
our charities, not because we wish to be praised for them, not because
we think they have great merit, but for our justification.   It is a capital
blunder ; as you discover, when another man recites his charities.

To speak the truth even with some austerity, to live with some
rigour of temperance or some extremes of generosity, seems to be an
asceticism which common good nature would appoint to those who are
at ease and in plenty, in sign that they feel a brotherhood with the great
multitude of suffering men.   And not only need we breathe and

exercise the soul by assuming the penalties of abstinence, of debt, of solitude, of unpopularity, but it behoves the wise man to look with a bold eye into those rarer dangers which sometimes invade men, and to familiarise himself with disgusting forms of disease, with sounds of execration, and the vision of violent death.

Times of heroism are generally times of terror ; but the day never shines in which this element may not work. The circumstances of man, we say, are historically somewhat better in this country, and at this hour, than perhaps ever before. More freedom exists for culture. It will not now run against an axe at the first step out of the beaten track of opinion. But whoso is heroic will always find cries to try his edge. Human virtue demands her champions and martyrs, and the trial of persecution always proceeds. It is but the other day that the brave Lovejoy gave his breast to the bullets of a mob for the rights of free speech and opinion, and died when it was better not to live.

I see not any road or perfect peace which a man can walk, but to take counsel of his own bosom. Let him quit too much association ; let him go home much, and establish himself in those courses he approves. The unremitting attention of simple and high sentiments in obscure duties is hardening the character to that temper which will work with honour, if need be, on the tumult or on the scaffold. Whatever outrages have happened to men may befall a man again ; and very easily in a republic, if there appear any signs of a decay of religion. Coarse slander, fire, tar and feathers, and the gibbet, the youth may freely bring home to his mind, and with what sweetness of temper he can, and inquire how fast he can fix his sense of duty, braving such penalties, whenever it may please the next newspaper, and a sufficient number of his neighbours, to pronounce his opinions incendiary.

It may calm the apprehension of calamity in the most susceptible heart, to see how quick a bound nature has set to the utmost infliction of malice. We rapidly approach a brink over which no enemy can follow us.

" Let them rave :

Thou art quiet in thy grave."

In the gloom of our ignorance of what shall be in the hour when we are deaf to the higher voices, who does not envy them who have seen safely to an end their manful endeavour ?   Who that sees the meanness of our politics, but inly congratulates Washington that he is long already wrapped in his shroud, and forever safe ; that he was laid sweet in his grave, the hope of humanity not yet subjugated in him ? Who does not sometimes envy the good and brave, who are no more to suffer from the tumults of the natural world, and await with curious complacency the speedy term of his own conversation with finite nature ?   And yet the love that will be annihilated sooner than treacherous, has already made death impossible, and affirms itself no mortal, but a native of the deeps of absolute and inextinguishable being.

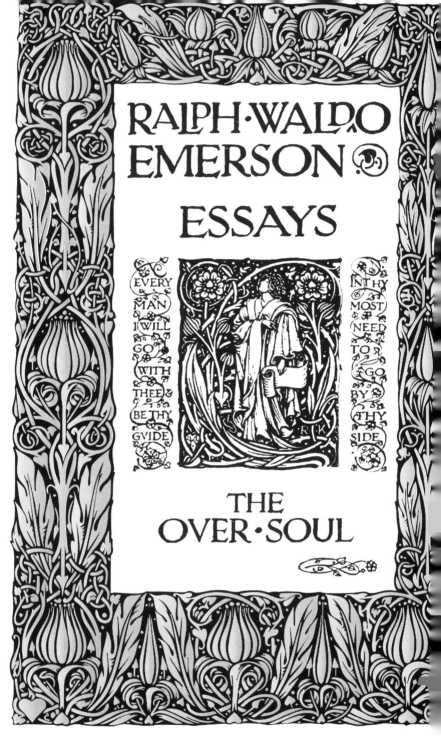

RALPH·WALDO
EMERSON

ESSAYS

EVERY MAN I WILL GO WITH THEE & BE THY GVIDE

INTHY MOST NEED TO GO BY THY SIDE

THE
OVER·SOUL

THE OVER-SOUL

" But souls that of his own good life partake

He loves as his own self ; dear as his eye

They are to Him : He'll never them forsake :

When they shall die, then God himself shall die :

They live, they live in blest eternity."

Henry More.

Edited by A.D Hendry
Cover Art by A.D Hendry

There is a difference between one and another hour of life in their authority and subsequent effect. Our faith comes in moments ; our vice is habitual. Yet is there a depth in those brief moments, which constrains us to ascribe more reality to them than to all other experiences. For this reason, the argument, which is always forthcoming to silence those who conceive extraordinary hopes of man, namely, the appeal to experience, is forever invalid and vain. A mightier hope abolishes despair. We give up the past to the objector, and yet we hope. He must explain this hope. We grant that human life is mean ; but how did we find out that it was mean ? What is the ground of this uneasiness of ours, of this old discontent ? What is the universal sense of want and ignorance, but the fine innuendo by which the great soul makes its enormous claim ? Why do men feel that the natural history of man has never been written, but always he is leaving behind what you have said of him, and it becomes old, and books of metaphysics worthless ? The philosophy of six thousand years has not searched the chambers and magazines of the soul. In its experiments there has always remained in the last analysis a residuum it could not resolve. Man is a stream whose source is hidden. Always our being is descending into us from we know not whence. The most exact calculator has no prescience that some-what incalculable may not baulk the very next moment. I am constrained every moment to acknowledge a higher origin for events than the will I call mine.

As with events, so it is with thoughts. When I watch that flowing river, which, out of regions I see not, pours for a season its streams into me,— I see that I am a pensioner,—not a cause, but a surprised spectator of this ethereal water ; that I desire and look up, and put myself in the attitude of reception, but from some alien energy the visions come.

The Supreme Critic on all the errors of the past and the present, and the only prophet of that which must be, is that great nature in

which we rest, as the earth lies in the soft arms of the atmosphere ; that
Unity, that Over-Soul, within which every man's particular being is
contained and made one with all other ; that common heart, of which
all sincere conversation is the worship, to which all right action is
submission ; that overpowering reality which confutes our tricks and
talents, and constrains every one to pass for what he is, and to speak
from his character and not from his tongue ; and which evermore tends
and aims to pass into our thought and hand, and become wisdom, and
virtue, and power, and beauty.   We live in succession, in division, in
parts, in particles.   Meantime, within man is the soul of the whole ; the
wise silence ; the universal beauty, to which every part and particle is
equally related ; the eternal *ONE.*   And this deep power in which we
exist, and whose beatitude is all accessible to us, is not only self-
sufficing and perfect in every hour, but the act of seeing and the thing
seen, the seer and the spectacle, the subject and the object, are one.
We see the world piece by piece, as the sun, the moon, the animal, the
tree ; but the whole, of which these are the shining parts, is the soul.
It is only by the vision of that Wisdom, that the horoscope of the ages
can be read, and it is only by falling back on our better thoughts, by
yielding to the spirit of prophecy which is innate in every man, that we
can know what it saith.   Every man's words, who speaks from that
life, must sound vain to those who do not dwell in the same thought on
their own part.   I dare not speak for it.   My words do not carry its
august sense ; they fall short and cold.   Only itself can inspire whom it
will, and behold, their speech shall be lyrical, and sweet, and universal
as the rising of the wind.   Yet I desire, even by profane words, if
sacred I may not use, to indicate the heaven of this deity, and to report
what hints I have collected of the transcendent simplicity and energy
of the Highest Law.

    If we consider what happens in conversation, in reveries, in
remorse, in times of passion, in surprises, in the instructions of dreams,
wherein often we see ourselves in masquerade,—the droll disguises
only magnifying and enhancing a real element, and forcing it on our
distinct notice,—we shall catch many hints that will broaden and

lighten into knowledge of the secret of nature. All goes to shew that the soul in man is not an organ, but animates and exercises all the organs ; is not a function, like the power of memory, of calculation, of comparison,—but uses these as hands and feet ; is not a faculty, but a light ; is not the intellect or the will, but the master of the intellect and the will ; is the vast background of our being, in which they lie,—an immensity not possessed and that cannot be possessed. From within or from behind, a light shines through us upon things, and makes us aware that we are nothing, but the light is all. A man is the façade of a temple, wherein all wisdom and all good abide. What we commonly call man,—the eating, drinking, planting, counting man,—does not, as we know him, represent himself, but misrepresents himself. Him we do not respect ; but the soul, whose organ he is, would let it reappear through his action, would make our knees bend. When it breathes through his intellect, it is genius ; when it breathes through his will, it is virtue ; when it flows through his affection, it is love. And the blindness of the intellect begins, when it would be something of itself. The weakness of the will begins, when the individual would be something of himself. All reform aims, in some one particular, to let the great soul have its way through us ; in other words, to engage us to obey.

Of this pure nature every man is at some time sensible. Language cannot paint it with his colours. It is too subtle. It is undefinable, unmeasurable ; but we know that it pervades and contains us. We know that all spiritual being is in man. A wise old proverb says, " God comes to see us without bell : " that is, as there is no screen or ceiling between our heads and the infinite heavens, so is there no bar or wall in the soul where man, the effect, ceases, and God, the cause, begins. The walls are taken away. We lie open on one side to the deeps of spiritual nature, to all the attributes of God. Justice we see and know, Love, Freedom, Power. These natures no man ever got above, but always they tower over us, and most in the moment when our interest tempt us to wound them.

The sovereignty of this nature whereof we speak is made known by its independency of those limitations which circumscribe us on every hand.   The soul circumscribeth all things.   As I have said, it contradicts all experience.   In like manner it abolishes time and space.   The influence of the senses has, in most men, over-powered the mind to that degree, that the walls of time and space have come to look solid, real, and insurmountable ; and to speak with levity of these limits is, in the world, the sign of insanity.   Yet time and space are but inverse measures of the force of the soul.   A man is capable of abolishing them both.   The spirit sports with time—

" Can crowd eternity into an hour,

Or stretch an hour to eternity"

We are often made to feel that there is another youth and age than that which is measured from the year of our natural birth.   Some thoughts always find us young, and keep us so.   Such a thought is the love of the universal and eternal beauty.   Every man parts from that contemplation with the feeling that it rather belongs to ages than to mortal life.   The least activity of the intellectual powers redeems us in a degree from the influences of time.   In sickness, in languor, give us a strain of poetry or a profound sentence, and we are refreshed ; or produce a volume of Plato or Shakespeare, or remind us of their names, and instantly we come into a feeling of longevity.   See how the deep, divine, thought demolishes centuries and millenniums and makes itself present through all ages.   Is the teaching of Christ less effective now than it was when first his mouth was opened ?   The emphasis of facts and persons to my soul's scale is one ; the scale of the senses and the understanding is another.   Before the great revelations of the soul, Time, Space, and Nature, shrink away.   In common speech, we refer all things to time, as we habitually refer the immensely sundered stars to one concave sphere.   And so we say that the Judgement is distant or near ; that the Millennium approaches ; that a day of certain political, moral, social reforms is at hand, and the like ; when we mean, that in the nature of things, one of the facts we contemplate is external and fugitive, and the other is permanent and collate with the soul. The things we now esteem fixed shall, one by one, detach landscape, the figures, Boston, London, are facts as fugitive as any institution past, or any whiff of mist or smoke, and so is society, and so is the world. The soul looketh steadily forwards, creating a world alway before her, and leaving worlds alway behind her. She has no dates, nor rites, nor persons, nor specialties, nor men. The soul knows only the soul. All else is idle weeds for her wearing.

After its own law, and not by arithmetic, is the rate of its progress to be computed. The soul's advances are not made by gradation, such as can be represented by motion in a straight line ; but rather by accession of state, such as can be represented by metamorphosis,— from the egg to the worm, form the worm to the fly. The growths of genius are of a certain *total* character, that does not advance the elect individual first over John, then Adam, then Richard, and give to each the pain of discovered inferiority, but by every throe of growth the man expands there where he works, passing, at each pulsation, classes, populations of men. With each divine impulse the mind rends the thin rinds of the visible and finite, and comes out into eternity's and inspires and expires its air. It converses with truths that have always been spoken in the world, and becomes conscious of a close sympathy with Zeno and Arrian than with persons in the house.

This is the law of moral and of mental gain. The simple rise as by specific levity, not into a particular virtue, but into the region of all the virtues. They are in the spirit which contains them all. The soul is superior to all the particulars of merit. The soul requires purity, but purity is not it ; requires justice, but justice is not that ; requires beneficence, but is somewhat better ; so that there is a kind of descent and accommodation felt when we leave speaking of moral nature, to urge a virtue which it enjoins. For to the soul in her pure action all the virtues are natural, and not painfully acquired. Speak to his heart, and the man becomes suddenly virtuous.

Within the same sentiment is the germ of intellectual growth, which obeys the same law. Those who are capable of humility, of justice, of love, of aspiration, are already on a platform that commands the sciences and arts, speech, and poetry, action and grace. For whoso dwells in this moral beatitude does already anticipate those special powers which men prize so highly ; just as love does justice to all the gifts of the object beloved. The lover has no talent, no skill, which passes for quite nothing with his enamoured maiden, however little she may possess of related faculty. And the heart, which abandons itself to the Supreme Mind, finds itself related to all its works, and will travel a royal road to particular knowledges and powers. For in ascending to this primary and aboriginal sentiment, we have come from our remote station on the circumference instantaneously to the centre of the world, where, as in the closet of God, we see causes, and anticipate the universe, which is but a slow effect.

One mode of the divine teaching is the incarnation of the spirit in a form,—in forms like my own. I live in society ; with persons who answer to thoughts in my own mind, or outwardly express to me a certain obedience to the great instincts to which I live. I see its presence to them. I am certified of a common nature ; and so these other souls, these separated slaves, draw me as nothing else can. They stir me in the new emotions we call passions ; of love, hatred, fear, admiration, pity ; thence comes conversation, competition, persuasion, cities, and war. Persons are supplementary to the primary teaching of the soul. In youth we are mad for persons. Childhood and youth see all the world in them. But the larger experience of man discovers the identical nature appearing through them all. Persons themselves acquaint us with the impersonal. In all conversation between two persons, tacit reference is made as to a third party, to a common nature. That third party or common nature is not social ; it is impersonal, is God. And so in groups where debate is earnest, and especially on great questions of thought, in which every heart beats with nobler sense of power and duty, and thinks and acts with unusual solemnity. All are conscious of attaining to a higher self-possession. It shines for all.   There is a certain wisdom of humanity which is common to the greatest men with the lowest, and which our ordinary education often labours to silence and obstruct.   The mind is one ; and the best minds, who love truth for its own sake, think much less of property in truth. Thankfully they accept it everywhere, and do not label or stamp it with any man's name, for it is theirs long before-hand.   It is theirs from eternity.   The learned and the studious of thought have no monopoly of wisdom.   Their violence of direction in some degree disqualifies them to think truly.   We owe many valuable observations to people who are not very acute or profound, and who say the thing without effort, which we want and have long been hunting in vain.   The action of the soul is oftener in that which is felt and left unsaid, than in that which is said in any conversation.   It broods over every society, and they unconsciously seek for it in each other.   We know better than we do.   We do not yet possess ourselves, and we know at the same time that we are much more.   I feel the same truth how often in my trivial conversation with my neighbours, that somewhat higher than each of us overlooks this by-play, and Jove nods to Jove from behind each of us.

Men descend to meet.   In their habitual and mean service to the world, for which they forsake their native nobleness, they resemble those Arabian Sheikhs, who dwell in mean houses, and effect an external poverty, to escape the rapacity of the Pasha, and reserve all their display of wealth for their interior and guarded retirements.

As it is present in all persons, so it is in every period of life.   It is adult already in the infant man.   In my dealing with my child, my Latin and Greek, my accomplishments and my money, stead me nothing.   They are all lost on him : but as much soul as I have avails. If I am merely wilful, he gives me a Rowland for an Oliver, sets his will against mine, one for one, and leaves me, if I please, the degradation of beating him by my superiority of strength.   But if I renounce my will, and act for the soul, setting that up as umpire between us two, out of his young eyes look the same soul ; he reveres and loves with me.

The soul is the perceiver and revealer of truth.   We know truth when we see it, let sceptic and scoffer say what they choose.   Foolish people ask you, when you have spoken what they do not wish to hear, " How do you know it is truth, and not an error of your own ?"   We know truth when we see it, from opinion, as we know when we are awake that we are awake.   It was a grand sentence of Emmanuel Swedenborg, which would alone indicate the greatness of that man's perception,— " It is no truth of a man's understanding to be able to affirm whatever he pleases ; but to be able to discern that what is true is true, and that what is false is false, this is the mark and character of intelligence."   In the book I read, the good thought returns to me, as every truth will, the image of the whole soul.   To the bad thought which I find in it, the same soul becomes a discerning, separating sword, and lops it away.   We are wiser than we know.   If we will not interfere with our thought, but will act entirely, or see how the thing stands in God, we know the particular thing, and every thing, and every man.   For the Maker of all things and persons stands behind us, and casts his dread omniscience through us over things.

But beyond this recognition of its own in particular passages of the individual's experience, it also reveals truth.   And here we should seek to reinforce ourselves by its very presence, and to speak with a worthier, loftier strain of that advent.   For the soul's communication of truth is the highest event in nature ; for it then does not give somewhat from itself, but it gives itself, or passes into and becomes that man whom it enlightens ; or in proportion to that truth he receives, it takes him to itself.

We distinguish the announcements of the soul, its manifestations of its own nature, by the term *Revelation*.   These are always attended by the emotion of the sublime.   For this communication is an influx of the Divine mind into our mind.   It is an ebb of the individual rivulet before the flowing surges of the sea of life.   Every distinct apprehension of this central commandment agitates men with awe and delight. A thrill passes through all men at the reception of new truth, or at the performance of a great action, which comes out of the heart of nature. In these communications, the power to see is not separated from the will to do, but the insight proceeds from obedience, and the obedience proceeds from a joyful perception. Every moment the individual feels himself invaded by it is memorable. Always, I believe, by the necessity of our constitution, a certain enthusiasm attends the individual's consciousness of that divine presence. The character and duration of this enthusiasm varies with the state of the individual, from an ecstasy and trance and prophetic inspiration, which is its rarer appearance, to the faintest glow of virtuous emotion, in which form it warms, like our household fires, all the families and associations of men, and makes society possible. A certain tendency to insanity has always attending the opening of this religious sense in men, as if " blasted with excess of light." The trances of Socrates ; the " union" of Plotinus ; the vision of Porphyry ; the conversion of Paul ; the aurora of Behmen ; the convulsions of George Fox and his Quakers ; the illumination of Swedenborg ; are of this kind. What was in the case of these remarkable persons a ravishment has in innumerable instances in common life been exhibited in less striking manner. Everywhere the history of religion betrays a tendency to enthusiasm. The rapture of the Moravian and Quietest ; the opening of the internal sense of the Word, in the language of the New Jerusalem Church ; the revival of the Calvinist Churches ; the experiences of the Methodists,— are varying forms of the shudder of awe and delight with which the individual soul always mingles with the universal soul.

The nature of these revelations is always the same. They are perceptions of the absolute law : they are solutions of the soul's own questions. They do not answer the questions which the understanding asks. The soul answers never by words, but by the thing itself that is inquired after.

Revelation is the disclosure of the soul.   The popular notion of a
revelation is, that it is a telling of fortunes.   In past oracles of the soul,
the understanding seeks to find answers to sensual questions, and
undertakes to tell from God how long men shall exist, what their hands
shall do, and who shall be their company, adding even names, and
dates and places.   But we must pick no locks.   We must check this
low curiosity.   An answer in words is delusive ; it is really no answer
to the questions you ask.   Do not ask a description of the countries
towards which you sail.   The description does not describe them to
you ; and to-morrow you arrive there, and know them by inhabiting
them.   Men ask of the immortality of the soul, and the employments
of heaven, and the state of the sinner, and so forth.   They even dream
that Jesus has left replies to precisely these interrogatories.   Never a
moment did that sublime spirit speak in their *patois.* To truth, justice,
love, the attributes of the soul, the idea of immutableness is essentially
associated.   Jesus, living in the moral sentiments, heedless of sensual
fortunes, heeding only the manifestations of these, never made the
separation of the idea of duration from the essence of these attributes ;
never uttered a syllable concerning the duration of the soul.   It was
left to his disciples to sever duration from the moral elements, and to
teach the immortality of the souls doctrine, and maintain it by
evidences.   The moment the doctrine of the immortality is separately
taught, man is already fallen.   In the flowing of love, the adoration of
humility, there is no question of continuance.   No inspired man ever
asks this question, or condescends to these evidences.   For the soul is
true to itself ; and the man in whom it is shed abroad cannot wander
from the present, which is infinite, to a future, which would be finite.

These questions which we lust to ask about the future are a
confession of sin.   God has no answer for them.   No answer in words
can reply to a question of things.   It is not in an arbitrary "decree of
God," but in the nature of man, that a veil shuts down on the facts of
to-morrow : for the soul will not have us read any other cipher but that
of cause and effect.   By this veil, which curtains events, it instructs the
children of men to live in to-day.   The only mode of obtaining an

answer to these questions of the senses, is to forego all low curiosity, and accepting the tide of being which floats us into the secret of nature, work and live, work and live, and all unawares the advancing soul has built and forged for itself a new condition, and the question and the answer are one.

Thus is the soul the perceiver and revealer of truth. By the same fire, serene, impersonal, perfect, which burns until it shall dissolve all things into the waves and surges of an ocean of light,—we see and know each other, and what spirit each is of. Who can tell the grounds of his knowledge of the character of the several individuals in his circle of friends ? No man. Yet their acts and words do not disappoint him. In that man, he knew no ill of him, he put no trust. In that other, though they had seldom met, authentic signs had yet passed to signify that he might be trusted as one who had an interest in his own character. We know each other very well,—which of us had been just to himself, and whether that with we teach or behold is only an inspiration, or is our honest effort also.

We are all discerners of spirits. That diagnoses lies aloft in our life or unconscious power, not in the understanding. The whole intercourse of society, its trade, its religion, its friendships, its quarrels, —is one wide judicial investigation of character. In full court, or in small committee, or confronted face to face, accuser and accused, men offer themselves to be judged. Against their will they exhibit those decisive trifles by which character is read. But who judges ? and what ? Not our understanding. We do not read them by learning or craft. No ; the wisdom of the wise man consists herein, that he does not judge them ; he lets them judge themselves, and merely reads and records their own verdict.

By virtue of this inevitable nature, private will is over-powered, and, maugre our efforts or our imperfections, your genius will speak from you, and mine from me. That which we are, we shall teach, not voluntarily, but involuntarily. Thoughts come into our minds by avenues which we never left open, and thoughts go out of our minds

through avenues which we never voluntarily opened.   Character
teaches over our head.   The infallible index of true progress is found
in the tone the man takes.   Neither his age, nor his breeding, nor
company, nor books, nor actions, nor talents, nor all together, can
hinder him from being deferential to a higher spirit than his own.   If
he have not found his home in God, his manners, his forms of speech,
the turn of his sentences, the build, shall I say, of all his opinions, will
involuntarily confess it, let him brave it out how he will.   If he have
found his centre, the Deity will shine through him, through all the
disguises of ignorance, of ungenial temperament, of unfavourable
circumstance.   The tone of seeking is one, and the tone of having is
another.

The great distinction between teachers sacred or literary, between
pets like Herbert, and poets like Pope ; between philosophers like
Spinoza, Kant, and, Coleridge,—and philosophers like Locke, Pale,
Mackintosh and Stewart ; between men of the world who are reckoned
accomplished talkers, and here and there a fervent mystic, prophesying
half-insane under the infinitude of his thought, is, that one class speak
from within, or from experience, as parties and possessors of the fact ;
and the other class, *from without,* as spectators merely, or perhaps as
acquainted with the fact on the evidence of third persons.   It is of no
use to preach to me from without.   I can do that too easily myself.
Jesus speak always from within, and in a degree that transcends all
others.   In that is the miracle.   That includes the miracle.   My soul
believe beforehand that it ought so to be.   All men stand continually in
the expectation of the appearance of such a teacher.   But if a man do
not speak from within the veil, where the word is one that it tells of, let
him lowly confess it.

The same Omniscience flows into the intellect, and makes what we
call genius.   Much of the wisdom of the world is not wisdom, and the
most illuminated class of men are no doubt superior to literary fame,
and are not writers.   Among the multitude of scholars and authors we
feel no harrowing presence ; we are sensible of a knack and skill rather

than of inspiration ; they have a light, and know not whence it comes, and call it their own ; their talent is some exaggerated faculty, some overgrown member, so that their strength is a disease. In these instances the intellectual gifts do not make the impression of virtue, but almost of vice ; and we feel that a man's talents stand in the way of his advancement in truth. But genius is religious. It is a larger imbibing of the common heart. It is not anomalous, but more like, and not less like, other men. There is in all great poets a wisdom of humanity, which is superior to any talents they exercise. The author, the wit, the partisan, the fine gentleman, does not take place of the man. Humanity shines in Homer, in Chaucer, in Spenser, in Shakespeare, in Milton. They are content with truth. They use the positive degree. They seem frigid and phlegmatic to those who have been spiced with the frantic passion and violent colouring of inferior, but popular writers. For they are poets by the free course which they allow to the informing soul, which through their eyes beholdeth again, and blesseth the things which it hath made. The soul is superior to its knowledge, wiser than any of its works. The great poet makes us feel our own wealth, and then we think less of his compositions. His greatest communication to our mind is, to teach us to despise all he has done. Shakespeare carries us to such a lofty strain of intelligent activity, as to suggest a wealth which beggars his own ; and we then feel that the splendid works which he has created, and which in other hours we extol as a sort of self-existent poetry, take no stronger hold of real nature than the shadow of a passing traveller on the rock. The inspiration which uttered itself in Hamlet and Lear could utter things as good from day to day forever. Why then should I make account of Hamlet and Lear, as if we had not the soul from which they fell as syllables from the tongue ?

This energy does not descend into individual life on any other condition than entire possession. It comes to the lowly and simple ; it comes to whomsoever will put off what is foreign and proud ; it comes as insight ; it comes as serenity and grandeur. When we see those whom it inhabits, we are apprised of new degrees of greatness. From that inspiration the man comes back with a changed tone. He does not talk with men with an eye to their opinion. He tries them. It requires of us to be plain and true. The vain traveller attempts to embellish his life by quoting my Lord, and the Prince, and the Countess, who thus said or did to *him*. The ambitious vulgar shew you their spoons, and brooches, and rings, and preserve their cards and compliments. The more cultivated, in their account of their own experience, cull out the pleasing poetic circumstance ; the visit to Rome ; the man of genius they saw ; the brilliant friend they know ; still further on, perhaps, the gorgeous landscape, the mountain lights, the mountain thoughts they enjoyed yesterday, —and so seek to throw a romantic colour over their life. But the soul that ascendith to worship the great God is plain and true ; has no rose-colour ; no fine friends ; no chivalry ; no adventures ; does not want admiration ; dwells in the hour that now is, in the earnest experience of the common day, —by reason of the present moment and the mere trifle having become porous to thoughts and bibulous of the sea of light.

Converse with a mind that is grandly simple, and literature looks like wood-catching. The simplest utterances are worthiest to be written, yet are they so cheap, and so things of course, that in the infinite riches of the soul, it is like gathering a few pebbles off the ground, or bottling a little air in a phial, when the whole earth and the whole atmosphere are ours. The mere author, in such society, is like a pickpocket among gentlemen, who has come in to steal a gold button or a pin. Nothing can pass there, or make you one of the circle, but the casting aside your trappings, and dealing man to man in naked truth, plain confession and omniscient affirmation.

Souls such as these treat you as gods would ; walk as gods in the earth, accepting without any admiration your wit, your bounty, your virtue even, say rather your act of duty, —for your virtue they own as their proper blood, royal as themselves, and over-royal, and the father of the gods. But what rebuke their plain fraternal bearing casts on the mutual flattery with which authors solace each other, and wound themselves ! These flatter not. I do not wonder that these men go to see Cromwell, and Christina, and Charles II., and James I., and the Grand Turk. For they are in their own elevation fellows of kings, and must feel the servile tone of conversation in the world. They must always be a godsend to princes, for they confront them, a king to a king, without duckling or concession, and give a high nature the refreshment and satisfaction of resistance, of plain humanity, of even companionship, and of new ideas. They leave them wiser and superior men. Souls like these make us feel that sincerity is more excellent than flattery. Deal so plainly with man and woman, as to contain the utmost sincerity, and destroy all hope of trifling with you. It is the highest compliment you can pay. Their "highest praising" said Milton, "is not flattery ; and their plainest advice is a kind of praising."

Ineffable is the union of man and God in every act of the soul. The simplest person, who in his integrity worships God, becomes God ; yet forever and ever the influx of this better and universal self is new and unsearchable ; ever it aspires awe and astonishment. How dear, how soothing to man, arises the idea of God peopling the lonely place, effecting the scar of our mistake and disappointments ! When we have broken our god of tradition, and ceased from our god of rhetoric, then may God fire the heart with his presence. It is the doubling of the heart itself, nay, the infinite enlargement of the heart with a power of growth to a new infinity on every side. It inspires in man an infallible trust. He has not the conviction, but the sight that the best is true, and may in that thought easily dismiss all particular uncertainties and fears, and adjourn to the sure revelation of time the solution of his private riddles. He is sure that his welfare is dear to the heart of being. In the presence of law to his mind, he is overflowed with a reliance so universal, that it sweeps away all cherished hopes and the most stable projects of mortal condition in its flood. He believes that he cannot escape from his good. The things that are really for thee gravitate to thee. You are running to seek your friend. Let your feet run, but your mind need not. If you do not find him, will you not acquiesce that it is best you should not find him ? for there is a power, which, as it is in you, is in him also, and could therefore very well bring you together, if it were for the best.   You are preparing with eagerness to go and render a service to which your talent and your taste invite you, the love of men, and the hope of fame. Has it not occurred to you, that you have no right to go, unless you are equally willing to be prevented from going ?   O believe, as thou livest, that eery sound that is spoken over the round world, which thou oughtest to hear, will vibrate on thine ear.   Every proverb, every book, every by-word that belongs to thee for aid or comfort, shall surely come home through open or winding passages.   Every friend whom not thy fantastic will, but the great and tender heart in thee craveth, shall lock thee in his embrace.   And this, because the heart in thee is the heart of all ; not a valve, not a wall, not an intersection is there anywhere in nature, but one blood rolled uninterruptedly, an endless circulation, through all men, as the water of the globe is all one sea, and, truly seen, its tide is one.

Let man, then, learn the revelation of all nature, and all thought to his heart ; this, namely, that the Highest dwells with him ; that the sources of nature are in his own mind, if the sentiment of duty is there. But if he would know what the great God speaketh, he must "go into his closet and shut the door," as Jesus said.   God will not make himself manifest to cowards.   He must greatly listen to himself, withdrawing himself from all the accents of other men's devotion. Their prayers even are hurtful to him, until he have made his own. The soul makes no appeal from itself.   Our religion vulgarly stands on numbers of believers.   Whenever the appeal is made,—no matter how indirectly,—to numbers, proclamation is then and there made, that religion is not.   He that finds God a sweet, enveloping thought to him, never counts his company.   When I sit in that presence, who shall dare to come in ?   When I rest in perfect humility, when I burn with pure love, what can Calvin or Swedenborg say ?

It makes no difference whether the appeal is to numbers or to one. The faith that stands on authority is not faith. The reliance on authority measures the decline of religion, the withdrawal of the soul. The position men have given to Jesus now for many centuries of history is a position of authority. It characterises themselves. It cannot alter the eternal facts. Great is the soul, and plain. It is no flatterer, it is no follower ; it never appeals from itself. It always believes in itself. Before the immense possibilities of man, all mere experience, all past biography, however spotless and sainted, shrinks away. Before that holy heaven which our presentiments foreshew us, we cannot easily praise any form of life we have seen or read of. We not only affirm that we have few great men, but, absolutely speaking, that we have none ; that we have no history, no record of any character or mode of living that entirely contents us. The saints and demigods whom history worships, we are strained to accept with a grain of allowance. Though in our lonely hours we draw a new strength out of their memory, yet pressed on our attention, as they are by the thoughtless and customary, they fatigue and invade. The soul gives itself alone, original and pure, to the Lonely. Original, and Pure, who, on that condition, gladly inhabits, leads, and speaks through it. Then it is glad, young, and nimble. It is not wise, but it see through all things. It is not called religious, but it is innocent. It calls the light its own, and feels that the grass grows and the stone falls by a law inferior to and dependent on its nature. Behold, it saith, I am born into the great, the universal mind. I the imperfect adore my own Perfect. I am somehow receptive of the great soul, and thereby, I do overlook the sun and the stars, and feel them to be but the fair accidents and effects which change and pass. More and more the surges of everlasting nature enter into me, and I become public and human in my regards and actions. So come I to live in thoughts, and act with energies which are immortal. Thus reeling the soul, and learning, as the ancient said, that " its beauty is immense," man will come to see that the world is the perineal miracle which the soul worketh, and be less astonished at particular wonders ; he will learn that there is no profane history ; that all history is sacred ; that the

universe is represented in an atom, in a moment of time.   He will no
longer weave a spotted life of shreds and patches, but he will live with
a divine unity.   He will cease from that base and frivolous in his own
life, and be content with all places and any service he can render.   He
will calmly front the morrow in the negligence of that trust which
carries God with it, and so hath already the whole future in the bottom
of the heart.

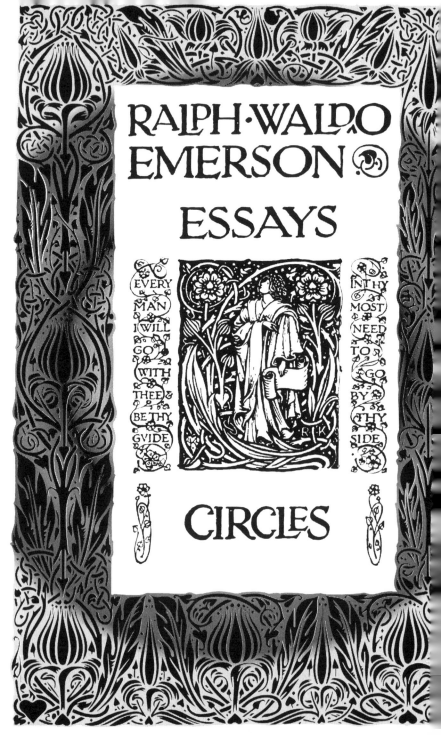

RALPH·WALDO EMERSON

ESSAYS

EVERY MAN I WILL GO WITH THEE & BE THY GVIDE

IN THY MOST NEED TO GO BY THY SIDE

CIRCLES

CIRCLES

Edited by A.D Hendry
Cover Art by A.D Hendry

The eye is the first circle ; the horizon which it forms is the second ; and throughout nature this primary figure is repeated without end.   It is the highest emblem in the cipher of the world.   St. Augustine described the nature of God as a circle whose centre was everywhere, and its circumference nowhere.   We are all our lifetime reading the copious sense of this first of forms.   One moral we have already deduced in considering the circular or compensatory character of every human action.   Another analogy we shall now trace,—that every action admits of being outdone.   Our life is an apprenticeship to the truth, that around every circle another can be drawn ; that there is no end in nature, but every end is a beginning ; that there is always another dawn risen on mid-noon, and under every deep a lower deep opens.

This fact, as far as is symbolises that moral fact of the Unattainable, the flying Perfect, around which the hands of man can never meet, at once the inspirer and condemner of every success, may conveniently serve us to connect many illustrations of human power in every department.

There are no fixtures in nature.   The universe is fluid and volatile. Permanence is but a word of degrees.   Our globe seen by God is a transparent law, not a mass of facts.   The law dissolves the fact and holds it fluid.   Our culture is the predominance of an idea which draws after it all this train of cities and institutions.   Let us rise into another idea, they will disappear.   The Greek sculpture is all melted away, as if it had been statues of ice, here and there a solitary figure or fragment remaining, as we see flecks and scraps of snow left in cold dells and mountain clefts in June and July.   For the genius that created it creates now somewhat else.   The Greek letters last a little longer, but are already passing under the same sentence, and tumbling into the inevitable pit which the creation of new thought opens for all that which is old.   The new continents are built out of the ruins of an old planet : the new races fed out of the decomposition of the foregoing. New arts destroy the old.   See the investment of capital in aqueducts made useless by hydraulics ; fortifications, by gunpowder ; roads and canals, by railways ; sails, by steam ; steam, by electricity.

You admire this tower of granite, weathering the hurts of so many ages. Yet a little waving hand built this huge wall, and that which builds is better than that which is built. The hand that built can topple it down much faster. Better than the hand, and nimbler, was the invisible thought which wrought through it ; and thus ever behind the coarse effect is a fine cause, which, being narrowly seen, is itself the effect of a finer cause. Every thing looks permanent until its secret is known. A rich estate appears to women and children a firm and lasting fact ; to a merchant, one easily created out of any materials, easily lost. An orchard, good tillage, good grounds, seem a fixture, like a gold mine or a river, to a citizen, but to a large farmer, not much more fixed than the state of the crop. Nature looks provokingly stable and secular, but is has a cause like all the rest ; and when once I comprehend that, will these fields stretch so immovably wide, these leaves hang so individually considerable ? Permanence is a word of degrees. Every thing is medial. Moons are no more bounds to spiritual power than bat-balls.

The key to every man is his thought. Sturdy and defying though he look, he has a helm which he obeys, which is, the idea after which all his facts are classified. He can only be reformed by shewing him a new idea which commands his own. The life of a man is a self-evolving circle, which, from a ring imperceptibly small, rushes on all sides outwards to new and larger circles, and that without end. The extent to which this generation of circles, wheel without wheel, will go, depends on the force or truth of the individual soul. For it is the inert effort of each thought, having formed itself into a circular way of circumstance,—as, for instance, an empire, rules of an art, a local usage, a religious rite,—to heap itself on that ridge, and to solidify, and hem in the life. But if the soul is quick and strong, it bursts over the boundary on all sides, and expands another on the great deep, which also runs up into a high wave, with attempt again to stop and bind.

But the heart refuses to be imprisoned ; in its first and narrowest pulse it already tends outward with a vast force, and to immense and innumerable expansions.

Every ultimate fact is only the first of a new series ; every general law only a particular fact of some more general law presently to disclose itself. There is no outside, no enclosing wall, no circumference to us. The man finishes his story,—how good ! how final ! how it puts a new face on all things ! He fills the sky. Lo, on the other side rises also a man, and draws a circle around the circle we had just pronounced the outline of the sphere. Then already is our first speaker not man, but only a first speaker. His only redress is forthwith to draw a circle outside of his antagonist. And so men do by themselves. The result of to-day, which haunts the mind and cannot be escaped, will presently be abridged into a word ; and the principle, that seems to explain nature, will itself be included as one example of a bolder generalisation. In the thought of to-morrow there is a power to upheave all of thy creed, all the creeds, all the literatures of the nations, and marshal thee to a heaven which no epic dream has yet depicted. Every man is not so much a workman in the world, as he is a suggestion of that he should be. Men walk as prophecies of the next age.

Step by step we scale this mysterious ladder : the steps are actions ; the new prospect is power. Every several result is threatened and judged by that which follows. Every one seems to be contradicted by the new ; it is only limited by the new. The new statement is always hated by the old, and, to those dwelling in the old, comes like an abyss of scepticism. But the eye soon gets wonted to it, for the eye and it are effects of one cause ; then its innocency and benefit appear, and presently, all its energy spent, it pales and dwindles before the revelation of the new hour.

Fear not the new generalisation. Does the fact look crass and material, threatening to degrade thy theory of sprit ? Resist it not ; it goes to refine and raise thy theory of matter just as much.

There are no fixtures to men, if we appeal to consciousness.   Every man supposes himself to be fully understood ; and if there is any truth in him, if he rests at last on the divine soul, I see not how it can be otherwise.   The last chamber, the last closet, he must feel, was never opened ; there is always a residuum unknown, unanalysable.   That is, every man believes that he has a greater possibility.

Our moods do not believe in each other.   To-day I am full of thoughts, and can write what I please.   I see no reason why I should not have the same thought, the same power of expression to-morrow. What I write, whilst I write it, seems the most natural thing in the world : but yesterday I saw a dreary vacuity in this direction in which now I see so much ; and a month hence, I doubt not, I shall wonder who he was that wrote so many continuous pages.   Alas for this infirm faith, this will not strenuous, this vast ebb of a vast flow !   I am God in nature ; I am a weed by the wall.

The continual effort to raise himself above himself, to work a pitch above his last height, betrays itself in a man's relations.   We thirst for approbation, yet cannot forgive the approver.   The sweet of nature is love ; yet if I have a friend, I am tormented by my imperfections.   The love of me accuses the other party.   If he were high enough to slight me, then I could love him, and rise by my affection to new heights.   A man's growth is seen in the successive choirs of his friends.   For every friend whom he loses for truth, he gains a better.   I thought, as I walked in the woods and mused on my friends, why should I play with them this game of idolatry ?   I know and see too well, when not voluntarily blind, the speedy limits of persons called high and worthy. Rich, noble, and great, they are by the literary of our speech ; but they are not thee !   Every personal consideration that we allow costs us heavenly state.   We sell the thrones of angels for a short and turbulent pleasure.

How often must we learn this lesson ?   Men cease to interest us when we find their limitation.   The only sin is limitation.   As soon as you once come up with a man's limitations, it is all over with him.

Has he talents ? has he enterprises ? has he knowledge ? it boots not. Infinitely alluring and attractive was he to you yesterday, a great hope, a sea to swim in ; now you have found his shores, found it a pond, and you care not if you never see it again.

Each new step we take in a thought reconciles twenty seemingly discordant facts, as expressions of one law. Aristotle and Plato are reckoned the respective heads of two schools. A wise man will see that Aristotle Platonises. By going one step further back in thought, discordant opinions are reconciled, by being seen to be extremes of one principle, and we can never go so far back as to preclude a still higher vision.

Beware when the great God lets loose a thinker on this planet. Then all things are at risk. It is as when a conflagration has broken out in a great city, and no man knows what is safe, or where it will end. There is not a piece of science, but its flank may be turned to-morrow ; there is not any literary reputation, not the so-called eternal names of fame, and may not be revised and condemned. The very hopes of man, the thoughts of his heart, the religion of nations, the manners and morals of mankind, are all at the mercy of a new generalisation. Generalisation is always a new influx of divinity into the mind. Hence the thrill that attends it.

Valour consists in the power of self-recovery, so that a man cannot have his flank turned, cannot be out-generalised, but put him where you will, he stands. This can only be his preferring truth to his past apprehension of truth, and his alert acceptance of it from whatever quarter ; the intrepid conviction that his laws, his relations to society, his Christianity, his world, may at any time be suspended and decease.

There are degrees in idealism. We learnt first to play with it academically ; as the magnet was once a toy. Then we see in the heyday of youth and poetry that it may be true, that it is true in gleams and fragments. Then its countenance waxes stern and grand, and we see that it must be true. It now shews itself ethical and practical. We learn that God *is* ; that he is in me ; and that all things are shadows of him. The idealism of Berkeley is only a crude statement of the idealism of Jesus, and that again is a crude statement of the fact that all nature is the rapid efflux of goodness executing and organising itself. Much more obviously is history and the state of the world at any one time directly dependent on the intellectual classification then existing in the minds of men. The things which are dear to men at this hour are so on account of the ideas which have emerged on their mental horizon, and which cause the present order of things, as a tree bears its apples. A new degree of culture would instantly revolutionise the entire system of human pursuits.

Conversation is a game of circles. In conversation we pluck up the *termini* which bound the common of silence on every side. The parties are not to be judged by the spirit they partake and even express under this Pentecost. To-morrow they will have receded from this high-water mark. To-morrow you shall find them stooping under the old packsaddles. Yet let us enjoy the cloven flame while it glows on our walls. When each new speaker strikes a new light, emancipates us from the oppression of the last speaker, to oppress us with the greatness and exclusiveness of his own thought, then yields us to another redeemer, we seem to recover our rights, to become men. O what truths, profound and executable only in ages and orbs, are supposed in the announcement of every truth ! In common hours society sits cold and statuesque. We all stand waiting, empty,— knowing, possibly, that we can be full, surrounded by mighty symbols which are not symbols to us, but prose and trivial toys. Then cometh the god, and converts the statues into fiery men, and by a flask of his eye burns up the veil which shrouded all things ; and the meaning of the very furniture, of cup and saucer, of chair and clock and tester, is manifest. The facts which loomed so large in the fogs of yesterday,— property, climate, breeding, personal beauty, and the like, have strangely changed their proportions. All that we reckoned settled shakes now and rattles ; and literature, cities, climates, regions, leave their foundations, and dance before our eyes. And yet here again see

the sweet circumscription.   Good as is discourse, silence is better, and
shames it.   The length of the discourse indicates the distance of
thought betwixt the speaker and the hearer.   If they were at a perfect
understanding in any part, no words would be necessary thereon.   If at
one in all parts, no words would be suffered.

Literature is a point outside of our hodiernal circle, through which
a new one may be described.   The use of literature is to afford us a
platform whence we may command a view of our present life, a
purchase by which we may move it.   We fill ourselves with ancient
learning ; install ourselves the best we can in Greek, in Punic, in
Roman houses, only that we may wiselier see French, English, and
American houses and modes of living.   In like manner, we see
literature best from the midst of wild nature, or from the din of affairs,
or from a high religion.   The field cannot be well seen from within the
field.   The astronomer must have his diameter of the earth's orbit as a
base to find a parallax of any star.

Therefore we value the poet.   All the argument, and all the
wisdom, is not in the encyclopaedia, or the treatise of metaphysics, or
the Body of Divinity, but in the sonnet or the play.   In my daily work I
incline to repeat my old steps, and do not believe in remedial force, in
the power of change and reform.   But some Petrarch or Ariosto, filled
with the new wine of his imagination, writes me an ode, or a brisk
romance, full of daring thought and action.   He smiles and arouses me
with his shrill tones, breaks up my whole chain of habits, and I open
my eye on my own possibilities.   He claps wings to the sides of all the
solid old lumber of the world, and I am capable once more of choosing
a straight path in theory and practice.

We have the same need to command a view of the religion of the
world.   We can never see Christianity from the catechism :—from the
pastures, from a boat in the pond, from amidst the songs of wood-
birds, we possibly may.   Cleansed by the elemental light and wind,
steeped in the sea of beautiful forms which the field offers us, we may
chance to cast a right glance back upon biography.   Christianity is

rightly dear to the best of mankind ; yet was there never a young philosopher whose breeding had fallen into the Christian church , by who that brave text of Paul's was not specially prized, " Then shall also the Son be subject unto Him who put all things under him, that God may be all in all." Let the claims and virtues of persons be never so great and welcome, the instinct of man presses eagerly onward to the impersonal and illimitable, and gladly arms itself against the dogmatism of bigots with this generous word, out of the book itself.

The natural world may be conceived of as a system of concentric circles ; and we now and then detect in nature slight dislocations, which apprise us that this surface on which we now stand is not fixed, but sliding. These manifold tenacious qualities, this chemistry and vegetation, these metals and animals, which seem to stand there for their own sake, are means and methods only, are words of God, and as fugitive to other words. Has the naturalist or chemist learned his craft, who has explored the gravity of atoms and the elective affinities, who has not yet discerned the deeper law whereof this is only a partial or approximate statement, namely, that like draws to like ; and that the goods which belong to you gravitate to you, and need not be pursued with pains and cost ? Yet is that statement approximate also, and not final. Omnipresence is a higher fact. Not through subtle, subterranean channels need friend and fact be drawn to their counterpart, but, rightly considered, these things proceed from the eternal generation of the soul. Cause and effect are two sides of one fact.

The same law of eternal procession ranges all that we call the virtues, and extinguishes each in the light of a better. The great man will not be prudent in the popular sense ; all his prudence will be so much deduction from his grandeur. But it behoves each to see when he sacrifices prudence, to what god he devotes it ; if to ease and pleasure, he had better be prudent still ; if to a great trust, he can well spare his mule and panniers who has a winged chariot instead. Geoffrey draws on his boots to go through the woods, that his feet may

be safer from the bites of snakes ; Aaron never thinks of such a peril.
In many years, neither is harmed by such an accident. Yet is seems to
me that every precaution you take against such an evil, you put
yourself into the power of the evil. I suppose that the highest
prudence is the lowest prudence. Is this too sudden a rushing from the
centre to the verge of our orbit ? Think how may times we shall fall
back into pitiful calculations, before we take up our rest in the great
sentiment, or make the verge of to-day the new centre. Besides, your
bravest sentiment is familiar to the humblest men. The poor and the
low have their way of expressing the last facts of philosophy as well as
you. " Blessed be nothing," and " the worse things are, the better they
are," are proverbs which express the transcendentalism of common
life.

   One man's justice is another man's injustice ; one man's beauty,
another's ugliness ; one man's wisdom, another's folly, as one beholds
the same objects from a higher point of view. One man thinks justice
consists in paying debts, and has no measure in his abhorrence of
another who is very remiss in this duty, and makes the creditor wait
tediously. But that second man has his one way of looking at things ;
asks himself, which debt must I pay first, the debt to the rich, or the
debt to the poor ? the debt of money, or the debt of thought to
mankind, of genius to nature ? For you, O broker, there is no other
principle but arithmetic. For me, commerce is of trivial import ; love,
faith, truth of character, the aspiration of man, these are sacred : nor
can I detach one duty, like you, from al other duties, and concentrate
my forces mechanically on the payment of moneys. Let me live
onward : you shall find that, though slower, the progress of my
character will liquidate all these debts without injustice to higher
claims. If a man should dedicate himself to the payment of notes,
would not this be injustice ? Owes he no debt but money ? And are
all claims on him to be postponed to a landlord's or banker's ?

   There is no virtue which is final ; all are initial. The virtues of
society are vices of the saint. The terror of reform is the discovery

that we must carry away our virtues, or what we have always esteemed such, into the same pit that has consumed our grosser vices.

" Forgive his crimes, forgive his virtues too,

Those smaller faults, half converts to the right."

It is the highest power of divine moments that they abolish our contritions also. I accuse myself of sloth and unprofitableness, day by day ; but when these waves of God flow into me, I no longer reckon lost time. I no longer poorly compute my possible achievement by what remains to me of the month or the year ; for these moments confer a sort of omnipresence and omnipotence, which asks nothing of duration, but sees that the energy of the mind is commensurate with the work to be done, without time.

And thus, O circular philosopher, I hear some reader exclaim, you have arrived at a fine pyrrhonism, at an equivalence and indifferency of all actions, and would fain teach us, that, *if we are true*, forsooth, our crimes may be lively stones out of which we shall construct the temple of the true God.

I am not careful to justify myself. I own I am gladdened by seeing the predominance of the saccharine principle throughout vegetable nature, and not less by beholding in morals that unrestrained inundation of the principle of good into every chink and hole that selfishness has left open, yea, into selfishness and sin itself ; so satisfactions. But lest I should mislead any, when I have my own head and obey my whims, let me remind the reader that I am only an experimenter. Do not set the least value on what I do, or the least discredit on what I do not, as if I pretended to settle anything as true or false. I unsettle all things. No facts are to me sacred, none are profane ; I simply experiment ; an endless seeker, with no Past at my back.

Yet this incessant movement and progression, which all things partake, could never become sensible to us, but by contrast to some principle of fixture or stability in the soul. Whilst the eternal generation of circles proceeds, the eternal generator abides. That central life is somewhat superior to creation, superior to knowledge and thought, and contains all its circles. Forever it labours to create a life and thought as large and excellent as itself ; but in vain ; for that which is made instructs how to make a better.

Thus there is no sleep, no pause, no preservation, but all things renew, germinate, and spring. Why should we import rags and relics into the new hour ? Nature abhors the old, and old age seems the only disease : all others run into this one. We call it by many names, fever, intemperance, insanity, stupidity, and crime : they are all forms of old age ; they are rest, conservatism, appropriation, inertia ; not newness, not the way onward. We grizzle every day. I see no need of it. Whilst we converse with what is above us, we do not grow old, but grow young. Infancy, youth, receptive, aspiring, with religious eye looking upward, counts itself nothing, and abandons itself to the instruction flowing from all sides. But the man and woman of seventy assume to know all ; throw up their hope ; renounce aspiration ; accept the actual from the necessary ; and talk down to the young. Let them then become organs of the Holy Ghost ; let them be lovers ; let them behold truth ; and their eyes are uplifted, their wrinkles smoothed, they are perfumed again with hope and power. This old age ought not to creep on a human mind. In nature every moment is new ; the past is always swallowed and forgotten ; the coming only is sacred. Nothing is secure but life, transition, the energising spirit. No love can be bound by oath or covenant, to secure it against a higher love. No truth so sublime but it may be trivial to-morrow in the light of new thoughts. People wish to be settled : only as far as they are unsettled, is there any hope for them.

Life is a series of surprises. We do not guess to-day the mood, the pleasure, the power of to-morrow, when we are building up our being. Of lower states,—of acts of routine and sense, we can tell somewhat ; but the masterpieces of God, the total growths and universal movements of the soul, he hideth ; they are incalculable. I can know that truth is divine and helpful ; but how it shall help me, I can have no guess, for *so to be* is the sole inlet of *so to know.* The new position of the advancing man has all the powers of the old, yet has them all new. It carries in its bosom all the energies of the past, yet is itself an exhalation of the morning. I cast away in this new moment all my once-hoarded knowledge, as vacant and vain. Now for the first time seem I to know any thing rightly. The simplest words,—we do not know what they mean, except when we love and aspire.

The difference between talents and character is adroitness to keep the old and trodden round, and power and courage to make a new road to new and better goals. Character makes an overpowering present, a cheerful determined hour, which fortifies all the company, by making them see that much is possible and excellent, that was not thought of. Character dulls the impression of particular events. When we see the conqueror, we do not think much of any one battle or success. We see that we had exaggerated the difficulty. It was easy to him. The great man is not convulsible or tormentable. He is so much, that events pass over him without much impression. People say sometimes, " See what I have overcome ; see how cheerful I am ; see how completely I have triumphed over these back events." Not if they still remind me of the black event,—they have not yet conquered. Is it conquest to be a gay and decorated sepulchre, or a half-crazed widow hysterically laughing ? True conquest is the causing the black event to fade and disappear, as an early cloud of insignificant result in a history so large and advancing.

The one thing which we seek with insatiable desire, is to forget ourselves, to be surprised out of propriety, without knowing how or why ; in short, to draw a new circle. Nothing great was ever achieved without enthusiasm.   The way of life is wonderful.   It is by abandonment.   The great moments of history are the facilities of performance through the strength of ideas, as the works of genius and religion.   " A man," said Oliver Cromwell, " never rises so high as when he know not whither he is going."   Dreams and drunkenness, the use of opium and alcohol, are the semblance and the counterfeit of this oracular genius, and hence their dangerous attraction of men.   For the like reason, they ask the aid of wild passions, as in gaming and war, to ape in some manner these flames and generosities of the heart.

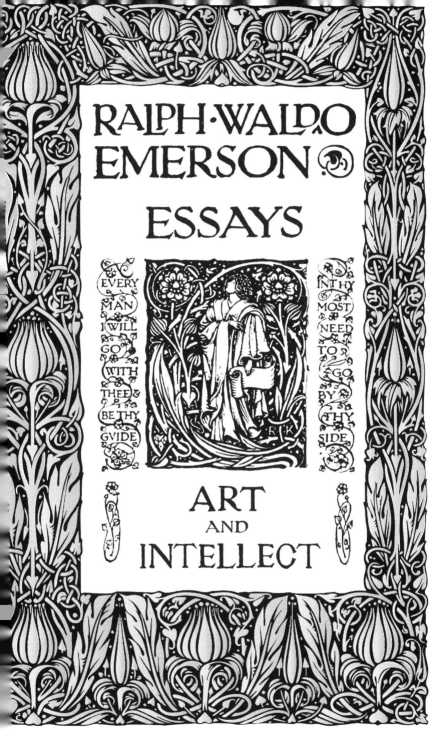

RALPH·WALDO EMERSON

ESSAYS

EVERY MAN I WILL GO WITH THEE & BE THY GVIDE

IN THY MOST NEED TO GO BY THY SIDE

ART
AND
INTELLECT

INTELLECT

Edited by A.D Hendry
Cover Art by A.D Hendry

Every substance is negatively electric to that which stands above it in the chemical tables, positively to that which stand below it. Water dissolves wood and stone and salt ; air dissolves water ; electric fire dissolves air ; but the intellect dissolves fire, gravity, laws, method, and the subtlest unnamed relations of nature, in its resistless menstruum. Intellect lies behind genius, which is intellect constructive. Intellect is the simple power anterior to all action or construction. Gladly would I unfold in calm degrees a natural history of the intellect ; but what man has yet been able to mark the steps and boundaries of that transparent essence ? The first questions are always to be asked ; and the wisest doctor is gravelled by the inquisitiveness of a child. How can we speak of the action of the mind under any divisions,—as, of its knowledge, of its ethics, of its works, and so forth,—since it melts will into perception, knowledge into act ? Each becomes the other. Itself alone is. Its vision is not like the vision of the eye, but is union with the things known.

Intellect and intellection signify, to the common ear, consideration of abstract truth. The consideration of time and place, of you and me, of profit and hurt, tyrannise over most men's minds. Intellect separates the fact considered from *you,* from all local and personal reference, and discerns it as if it existed for its own sake. Heraclitus looked upon the affections as dense and coloured mists. In the fog of good and evil affections, it is hard for man to walk forward in a straight line. Intellect is void of affection, and sees an object as if it stands in the light of science, cool and disengaged. The intellect goes out of the individual, floats over its own personality, and regards it as a fact, and not as *I* and *mine.* He who is immersed in what concerns person or place cannot see the problem of existence. This the intellect always ponders. Nature shews all things formed and bound. The intellect pierces the form, overleaps the wall, detects intrinsic likeness between remotes things, and reduces all things into a few principles.

The making a fact the subject of thought raises it. All that mass of mental and moral phenomena which we do not make objects of voluntary thought come within the power of fortune ; they constitute the circumstance of daily life ; they are subject to change, to fear, and hope. Every man beholds his human condition with a degree of melancholy. As a ship aground is battered by the waves, so man, imprisoned in mortal life, lies open to the mercy of coming events. But a truth, separated by the intellect, is no longer a subject of destiny. We behold it as a god upraised above care and fear. And so any fact in our life, or any record of our fancies or reflections, disentangled from the web of our unconsciousness, becomes an object impersonal and immortal. It is the past restored, but embalmed. A better art than that of Egypt has taken fear and corruption out of it. It is eviscerated of care. It is offered for science. What is addressed to us for contemplation does not threaten us, but makes us intellectual beings.

The growth of the intellect is spontaneous in every step. The mind that grows could not predict the times, the means, the mode of that spontaneity. God enters by a private door into every individual. Long prior to the age of refection is the thinking of the mind. Out of darkness it came insensibly into the marvellous light of to-day. Over it always reigned a firm law. In the period of infancy it accepted and disposed of all impressions from the surrounding creation after its own way. Whatever any mind doth or saith is after a law. It has no random act or word. And this native law remains over it after it has come to reflection or conscious thought. In the most worn, pedantic, introverted self-tormentor's life, the greatest part is incalculable by him, unforeseen, unimaginable, and must be, until he can take himself up by his own ears. What am I ? What has my will done to make me that I am ? Nothing. I have been floated into this thought, this hour, this connexion of events, by might and mind sublime, and my ingenuity and wilfulness have not thwarted, have not aided to an appreciable degree.

Our spontaneous action is always the best. You cannot, with your best deliberation and heed, come close to any questions as your spontaneous glance shall bring you, whilst you rise from your bed, or walk abroad in the morning, after meditating the matter before sleep on the previous night. Always our thinking is a pious reception. Our truth of thought is therefore vitiated as much by too violent direction given by our will, as by too great negligence. We do not determine what we will think. We only open our senses, clear away, as we can, all obstruction from the fact, and suffer the intellect to see. We have little control over our thoughts. We are the prisoners of ideas. They catch us up for moments into their heaven, and so fully engage us, that we take no thought for the morrow, gaze like children, without an effort to make them our own. By and by we fall out of that rapture, bethink us where we have been, what we have seen, and repeat, as truly as we can, what we have beheld. As far as we can recall these ecstasies, we carry away in ineffaceable memory the result, and all men and all ages confirm it. It is called truth. But the moment we cease to report it, and attempt to correct and contrive, it is not truth.

If we consider what persons have stimulated and profited us, we shall perceive the superiority of the spontaneous or intuitive principle over the arithmetical or logical. The first alway contains the second, but virtual and latent. We want in every man a long logic ; we can't pardon the absence of it, but it must not be spoken. Logic is the procession or proportionate unfolding of the intuition ; but its virtue is as silent method ; the moment it would appear as propositions, and have a separate value, it is worthless.

In every man's mind some images, words, and facts remain, without effort on his part to imprint them, which others forget, and afterwards these illustrate to him important laws. All our progress is an unfolding, like the vegetable bud. You have first an instinct, then an opinion, then a knowledge, as the plant has root, bud, and fruit. Trust the instinct to the end, though you can render no reason. It is vain to hurry it. By trusting it to the end, it shall ripen into truth, and you shall know why you believe.

Each mind has its own method. A true man never acquires after college rules. What you have aggregated in a natural manner surprises and delights when it is produced.   For we cannot oversee each other's secret.   And hence the differences between men in natural endowment are insignificant in comparison with their common wealth. Do you think the porter and the cook have no anecdotes, no experiences, no wonders for you ?   Every body knows as much as the savant.   The walls of rude minds are scrawled all over with facts, with thoughts.   They shall one day bring a lantern and read the inscriptions. Every man, in the degree in which he has wit and culture, finds his curiosity inflamed concerning the modes of living and thinking of other men, and especially of those classes whose minds have not been subdued by the drill of school education.

This instinctive action never ceases in a healthy mind, but becomes richer and more frequent in its informations through all states of culture.   At last comes the era of reflection, when we not only observe, but take pains to observe ; when we of set purpose sit down to consider an abstract truth ; when we keep the mind's eye open, whilst we conserve, whilst we read, whilst we act, intent to learn the secret law of some class of facts.

What is the hardest task in the world ?   To think.   I would put myself in the attitude to look in the eye an abstract truth, and I cannot. I blanch and withdraw on this side and that.   I seem to know what he meant who said, " No man can see God face to face and live."   For example, a man explores the basis of civil government.   Let him intend his mind without respite, without rest, in one direction.   His best heed long time avails him nothing.   Yet thoughts are flitting before him.   We all but apprehend, we dimly forebode the truth.   We say, I will walk abroad, and the truth will take form and clearness to me.   We go forth, but cannot find it.   It seems as if we need only the stillness and composed attitude of the library to seize the thought.   But we come in, and are as far from it as at first.   Then, in a moment, and unannounced, the truth appears.   A certain wandering light appears, and is the distinction, the principle we wanted.   But the oracle comes, because we had previously laid siege to the shrine.   It seems as if the law of the intellect resembled that law of nature by which we now inspire, now expire breath ; by which the heart now draws in, then hurls out the blood,—the law of undulation. So now you must labour with your brains, and now you must forbear your activity, and see what the great Soul sheweth.

Our intellections are mainly prospective. The immortality of man is as legitimately preached from the intellections as from the moral volitions. Every intellection is mainly prospective. Its present value is its least. It is a little seed. Inspect what delights you in Plutarch, in Shakespeare, in Cervantes. Each truth that a writer acquires is a lantern which he instantly turns full on what facts and thoughts lay already in his mind, and behold, all the mats and rubbish which had littered his garret become precious. Every trivial fact in his private biography becomes an illustration of this new principle, revisits the day, and delights all men by its piquancy and new charm. Men say, Where did he get this ? and think there was something divine in his life. But no ; they have myriads of facts just as good, would they only get a lamp to ransack their attics withal.

We are all wise. The difference between persons is not in wisdom, but in art. I knew, in an academical club, a person who always deferred to me, who, seeing my whim for writing, fancied that my experiences had somewhat superior ; whilst I saw that his experiences were as good as mine. Give them to me, and I would make the same use of them. He held the old ; he holds the new ; I had the habit of tacking together the old and the new ; which he did not use to exercise. This may hold in the great examples. Perhaps if we should meet Shakespeare, we should not be conscious of any steep inferiority ; no ; but of a great equality,—only that he possessed a strange skill of using, of classifying his facts, which we lacked. For, notwithstanding our utter incapacity to produce any thing like Hamlet and Othello, see the perfect perception this wit, and immense knowledge of life, and liquid eloquence, find in us all.

If you gather apples in the sunshine, or make hay, or hoe corn, and then retire within doors, and shut your eyes, and press them with your hand, you shall still see apples hanging in the bright light, with boughs and leaves thereto, or the tasselled grass, or the corn-flags ; and this for five or six hours afterwards.   There lie the impressions on the retentive organ, though you knew it not.   So lies the whole series of natural images with which your life has made you acquainted in your memory, though you know it not ; and a thrill of passion flashes light on their dark chamber, and the active power seizes instantly the fit image, as the word of its momentary thought.

It is long ere we discover how rich we are.   Our history, we are sure, is quite tame.   We have nothing to write, nothing to infer.   But our wiser years still run back to the despised recollections of childhood, and always we are fishing up some wonderful article out of that pond ; until, by and by, we begin to suspect that the biography of the one foolish person we know is, in reality, nothing less than the miniature paraphrase of the hundred volumes of the Universal History.

In the intellect constructive, which we popularly designate by the word Genius, we observe the same balance of two elements as in intellect receptive.   The constructive intellect produces thoughts, sentences, poems, plans, designs, systems.   It is the generation of the mind, the marriage of thought with nature.   To genius must always go two gifts, the thought and the publication.   The first is revelation, always a miracle, which no frequency of occurrence or incessant study can ever familiarise, but which must always leave the inquirer stupid with wonder.   It is the advent of truth into the world ; a form of thought now for the the first time bursting into the universe ; a child of the old eternal soul ; a piece of genuine and immeasurable greatness. It seems, for a time, to inherit all that has yet existed, and to dictate to the unborn.   It affects every thought of man, and goes to fashion every institution.   But to make it available, it needs a vehicle of art by which it is conveyed to men.   To be communicable, it must become picture or sensible object.   We must learn the language of facts.   The most wonderful inspirations die with their subject, if he has no hand to paint them to the senses. The ray of light passes invisible through space, and only when it falls on an object is it seen. When the spiritual energy is directed on something outward, then it is a thought. The relation between it and you first makes you, the value of you, apparent to me. The rich inventive genius of the painter must be smothered and lost for want of the power of drawing ; and in our happy hours we should be inexhaustible poets, if once we could break through the silence into adequate rhyme. As all men have some access to primary truth, so all have some art or power of communication in their hand. There is an inequality, whose laws we do not yet know, between two men and between two moments of the same man, in respect to this faculty. In common hours we have the same facts as in the uncommon or inspired ; but they do not sit for their portraits, they are not detached, but lie in a web. The thought of genius is spontaneous ; but the power of picture or expression, is the most enriched and flowing nature, implies a mixture of will, a certain control over the spontaneous states, without which no production is possible. It is a conversion of all nature into the rhetoric of thought, under the eye of judgement, with a strenuous exercise of choice. And yet the imaginative vocabulary seems to be spontaneous also. It does not flow from experience only or mainly, but from a richer source. Not by any conscious imitation of particular forms are the grand strokes of the painter executed ; but by repairing to the fountain-head of all forms in his mind. Who is the first drawing-master ? Without instruction we know very well the ideal of the human form. A child knows if an arm or a leg be distorted in a picture, if the attitude be natural, or grand, or mean, though he has never received any instruction in drawing, or heard any conversation on the subject, nor can himself draw with correctness a single figure. A good form strikes all eyes pleasantly long before they have any science on the subject ; and a beautiful face sets twenty hearts in palpitation prior to all consideration, of the mechanical proportions of the features and head. We may owe to dreams some light on the fountain of this skill ; for as soon as we let our will go, and let the the unconscious states ensue, see what cunning draughtsmen we are ! We entertain ourselves with wonderful forms of men, of women, of animals, of gardens, of woods, and of monsters ; and the mystic pencil wherewith we then draw has no awkwardness or inexperience, no meagreness or poverty ; it can design well and group well ; its composition is full of art, its colours are well laid on, and the whole canvas which it paints is life-like, and apt to touch us with terror, with tenderness, with desire, and with grief. Neither are the artist's copies from experience ever mere copies, but always touched and softened by tints from this ideal domain.

The conditions essential to a constructive mind do not appear to be so often combined but that a good sentence or verse remains fresh and memorable for a long time. Yet when we write with ease, and come out into the free air of thought, we seem to be assured that nothing is easier than to continue this communication at pleasure. Up, down, around, the kingdom of thought has no enclosures, but the Muse makes us free of her city. Well, the world has a million writers. One would think, then, that good thought would be as familiar as air and water, and the gifts of each new hour would exclude the last. Yet we can count all our good books ; nay, I remember any beautiful verse for twenty years. It is true that the discerning intellect of the world is always greatly in advance of the creative, so that always there are many competent judges of the same book, and few writers of the best books. But some of the conditions of intellectual construction are of rare occurrence. The intellect is a whole, and demands integrity in every work. This is resisted equally by a man's devotion to a single thought, and by his ambition to combine too many.

Truth is our element of life ; yet if a man fasten his attention on a single aspect of truth, and apply himself to that alone for a long time, the truth becomes distorted, and not itself, but falsehood ; herein resembling the air, which is our natural element, and the breath of our nostrils ; but if a stream of the same be directed on the body for a time, it causes cold, fever, and even death. How wearisome the grammarian, the phrenologist, the political or religious fanatic, or indeed any possessed mortal, whose balance is lost by the exaggeration of a single topic ! It is incipient insanity. Every thought is a prison also. I cannot see what you see, because I am caught up by a strong wind, and blown so far in one direction, that I am out of the hoop of your horizon.

Is it any better, if the student, to avoid this offence and to liberalise himself, aims to make a mechanical whole of history, or science, or philosophy, by a numerical addition of all the facts that fall within his vision ? The world refuses to be analysed by addition and subtraction. When we are young, we spend much time and pains in filling our note-books with all definitions of Religion, Love, Poetry, Politics, Art, in the hope that in the course of a few years we shall have condensed into our encyclopaedia the net value of all the theories at which the world has yet arrived. But year after year our tables get no completeness ; and at last we discover that our curve is a parabola, whose arcs will never meet.

Neither by detachment, neither by aggregation, is the integrity of the intellect transmitted to its works, but by a vigilance which brings the intellect in its greatness and best state to operate every moment. It must have the same wholeness nature has. Although no diligence can build the universe in a model, by the best accumulation or disposition of details, yet does the world reappear miniature in every event, so that all the laws of nature may be read in the smallest fact. The intellect must have the like perfection in its apprehension and its works. For this reason, an index or mercury of intellectual proficiency is the perception of identity. We talk with accomplished persons who appear to be strangers in nature. The cloud, the tree, the turf, the bird, are not theirs, have nothing of them ; the world is only their lodging and table. But the poet, whose verses are to be spheral and complete, is one whom nature cannot deceive, whatsoever face of strangeness she may put on. He feels a strict consanguinity, and detects more likeness than variety in all her changes. We are stung by the desire for new thought ; but when we receive a new thought, it is only the old thought with a new face ; and though we make it our own, we instantly crave another ; we are not really enriched. For the truth was in us before it was reflected to us from natural objects ; and the profound genius will cast the likeness of all creatures into every product of his wit.

But if the constructive powers are rare, and it is given to few men to be poets, yet every man is a receiver of this descending Holy Ghost, and may well study the laws of its influx. Exactly parallel is the whole rule of intellectual duty to the role of moral duty. A self-denial no less austere than the saint's is demanded of the scholar. He must worship truth, and forego all things for that, and choose defeat and pain, so that his treasure in thought is thereby augmented.

God offers to every mind its choice between truth and repose. Take which you please, —you can never have both. Between these, as a pendulum, man oscillates ever. He in whom the the love of repose predominates will accept the first creed, the first philosophy, the first political party he meets, —most likely his father's. He gets rest, commodity, and reputation ; but he shuts the door of truth. He in whom the love of truth predominates will keep himself aloof from all moorings and afloat. He will abstain from dogmatism, and recognise all the opposite negations between which, as walls, his being is swung. He submits to the inconvenience of suspense and imperfect opinion ; but he is a candidate for truth, as the other is not, and respects the highest law of his being.

The circle of the green earth he must measure with his shoes to find the man who can yield him truth. He shall then know that there is somewhat more blessed and great in hearing than in speaking. Happy is the hearing man ; unhappy the speaking man. As long as I hear truth, I am bathed by a beautiful element, and am not conscious of any limits to my nature. The suggestions are thousandfold that I hear and see. The waters of the great deep have ingress and egress to the soul. But if I speak, I define, I confine, and am less. When socrates speaks, Lysis and Menexenus are afflicted by no shame that they do not speak.

They also are good. He likewise defers to them, loves them, while he speaks. Because a true and natural man contains and is the same truth which an eloquent man articulates ; but in the eloquent man, because he can articulate it, it seems something the less to reside, and he turns to these silent beautiful with the more inclination and respect. The ancient sentence said, Let us be silent, for so are the gods. Silence is a solvent that destroys personality, and gives us leave to be great and universal. Every man's progress is through a succession of teachers, each of whom at the time seems to have a superlative influence, but it at last give place to a new. Frankly let him accept it all. Jesus says, Leave father, mother, house and lands, and follow me. Who leaves all receives more. This is true intellectually as morally. Each new mind we approach seems to require an abdication of all our past and present possessions. A new doctrine seems, at first, a subversion of all our opinions, tastes, and manner of living. Such has Swedenborg, such has Kant, such has Coleridge, such has Cousin, seemed to many young men in this country. Take thankfully and heartily all they can give. Exhaust them, wrestle with them, let them not go until their blessing be won ; and after a short season the dismay will be over-past, the excess of influence withdrawn, and they will be no longer an alarming meteor, but one more bright star shining serenely in your heaven, and blending its light with all your day.

But whilst he gives himself up unreservedly to that which draws him, because that is his own, he is to refuse himself to that which draws him not, whatsoever fame and authority may attend it, because it is not his own. Entire self-reliance belongs to the intellect. One soul is a counterpoise of all souls, as a capillary column of water is a balance for the sea. It must treat things, and books, and sovereign genius, as itself also a sovereign. If Æschylus be that man he is taken for, he has not yet done his office when has educated the learned of Europe for a thousand years. He is now to approve himself a master of delight to me also. If he cannot do that, all his fame shall avail him nothing with me. I were a fool not to sacrifice a thousand Æschyluses to my intellectual integrity. Especially take the same ground in regard to abstract truth, the science of the mind.   The Bacon, the Spinoza, the Hume, Schelling, Kant, or whosoever propounds to you a philosophy of the mind, is only a more or less awkward translator of things in your consciousness, which you have also your way of seeing, perhaps of denominating.   Say then, instead of too timidly poring into this obscure sense, that he has not succeeded in rendering back to you your consciousness.   He has not succeeded ; now let another try.   If Plato cannot, perhaps Spinoza will.   If Spinoza cannot, then perhaps Kant. Any how, when at last it is done, you will find it is no recondite, but a simple, natural, common state, which the writer restores to you.

But let us end these didactics.   I will not, though the subject might provoke it, speak to the open question between Truth and Love.   I shall not presume to interfere in the old politics of the skies ; " The cherubim know most ; the seraphim love most."   The gods shall settle their own quarrels.   But I cannot recite, even thus rudely, laws of the intellect, without remembering that lofty and sequestered class of men who have been its prophets and oracles, the high priesthood of the pure reason, the *Trismegisiti,* the expounders of the principles of thought from age to age.   When, at long intervals, we turn over these abstruse pages, wonderful seems the calm and grand air of these few, these great spiritual lords, who have walked in the world,—these of the old religion,—dwelling in a worship which makes the sanctities of christianity look *parvenues* and popular ; for " persuasion is in soul, but necessity is in intellect."   This band of grandees, Hermes, Heraclitus, Empedocles, Plato, Plotinus, Olympiodorus, Proclus, Synesius, and the rest, have somewhat so vast in their logic, so primary in their thinking, that it seems antecedent to all the ordinary distinctions of rhetoric and literature, and to be at once poetry, and music, and dancing, and astronomy, and mathematics.   I am present at the sowing of the seed of the world.   With a geometry of sunbeams, the soul lays foundations of nature.   The truth and grandeur of their thought is proved by its scope and applicability ; for it commands the entire schedule and inventory of things for its illustration.   But what marks its elevation, and has even a comic look to us, is the innocent serenity with which these babe-like Jupiters sit in their clouds, and from age to age prattle to each other, and to no contemporary. Well assured that their speech is intelligible, and the most natural thing in the world, they add thesis to thesis, without a moment's heed of the universal astonishment of the human race below, who do not comprehend their plainest argument ; nor do they ever relent so much as to insert a popular or explaining sentence ; nor testify the least displeasure or petulance at the dullness of their amazed auditory. The angels are so enamoured of the language that is spoken in heaven, that they will not distort their lips with the hissing and unmusical dialects of men, but speak their own, whether there be any who understand it or not.

ART

Edited by A.D Hendry
Cover Art by A.D Hendry

Because the soul is progressive, it never quite repeats itself, but in every act attempts the production of a new and fairer whole. This appears in works of both the useful and the fine arts, if we employ the popular distinction of works according to their aim, either at use or beauty. Thus in our fine arts, not imitation, but creation is the aim. In landscapes, the painter should give the suggestion of a fairer creation than we know. The details, the prose of nature, he should omit, and give us only the spirit and splendour. He should know that the landscape has beauty for his eye, because it expresses a thought which is to him good : and this, because the same power which sees through his eyes is seen in that spectacle ; and he will come to value the expression of nature, and not nature itself, and so exalt in his copy the features that please him. He will give the gloom of gloom, and the sunshine of sunshine. In a portrait he must inscribe the character, and not the features, and must esteem the man who sits to him as himself only an imperfect picture or likeness of the aspiring original within.

What is that abridgement and selection we observe in all spiritual activity, but itself the creative impulse ? for it is the inlet of that higher illumination which teaches to convert a larger sense by simpler symbols. What is a man but nature's finer success in self-explication ? What is a man but a finer and compacter landscape than the horizon figures,—nature's eclecticism ? and what is his speech, his love of painting, love of nature, but still a finer success,—all the weary miles and tones of space and bulk left out, and the spirit or moral of it contracted into a musical word, or the most cunning stroke of the pencil ?

But the artist must employ the symbols in use in his day and nation to convey his enlarged sense to his fellow-men. Thus the new in art is always formed out of the old. The Genius of the Hour always sets his ineffaceable seal on the work, and gives it an inexpressible charm for the imagination. As far as the spiritual character of the period overpowers the artist and finds expression in his work, so far it will always retain a certain grandeur, and will represent to future holders the Unknown, the Inevitable, the Divine. No man can quite exclude this element of Necessity from his labour. No man can quite emancipate himself from his age and his country, or produce a model in which the education, the religion, the politics, usages, and arts of his times shall have no share. Though he were never so original, never so wilful and fantastic, he cannot wipe out of his work every trace of the thoughts amidst which it grew. The very avoidance betrays the usage he avoids. Above his will, and out of his sight, he is necessitated, by the air he breathes, and the idea on which his contemporaries live and toil, to share the manner of his times, without knowing what that manner is. Now that which is inevitable in the work has a higher charm than individual talent can ever give, inasmuch as the artist's pen or chisel seems to have been held and guided by a gigantic hand to inscribe a line in the history of the human race. The circumstance gives a value to the Egyptian hieroglyphics, to the Indian, Chinese, and Mexican idols, however gross and shapeless. They denote the height of the human soul in that hour, and were not fantastic, but sprung from a necessity as deep as the world. Shall I now add, that the whole extant product of the plastic arts has herein its highest value as *history* ; as a stroke drawn in the portrait of that fate, perfect and beautiful, according to whose ordinations all beings advance to their beatitude.

Thus, historically viewed, it has been the office of art to educate the perception of beauty. We are immersed in beauty, but our eyes have no clear vision. It needs, by the exhibition of single traits, to assist and lead the dormant taste. We carve and paint, or we behold what is carved and painted, as students of the mystery of Form. The virtue of art lies in detachment, in sequestering one object from the embarrassing variety. Until one thing comes out from the connexion of things, there can be enjoyment, contemplation, but no thought. Our happiness and unhappiness are unproductive. The infant lies in a pleasing trance ; but his individual character and his practical power depend on his daily progress in the separation of things, and dealing with one at a time. Love and all the passions concentrate all existence around a single form.   It is the bait of certain minds to give an all-excluding fulness to the object, the thought, the word, they alight upon, and to make that for the time the deputy of the world.   These are the artists, the orators, the leaders of society.   The power to detach, and to magnify by detaching, is the essence of rhetoric in the hands of the orator and the poet.   This rhetoric, or power to fix the momentary eminency of an object,—so remarkable in Burke, in Byron, in Carlyle, —the painter and sculptor exhibit in colour and in stone.   The power depends on the depth of the artist's insight of that object he contemplates.   For every object has its roots in central nature, and may of course be so exhibited to us as to represent the world.   Therefore each work of genius is the tyrant of the hour, and concentrates attention on itself.   For the time, it is the only thing worth naming, to do that,—be it a sonnet, an opera, a landscape, a statue, an oration, the plan of a temple, of a campaign, or of a voyage of discovery.   Presently we pass to some other object, which rounds itself into a whole, as did the first ; for example, a well-laid garden,—and nothing seems worth doing but the laying out of gardens.   I should think fire the best thing in the world, if I were not acquainted with air, and water, and earth.   For it is the right and property of all natural objects, of all genuine talents, of all native properties whatsoever, to be for their moment the top of the world.   A squirrel leaping from bough to bough, and making the wood but one wide tree for his pleasure, fills the eye not less than a lion, is beautiful, self-sufficing, and stands then and there for nature.   A good ballad draws my ear and heart whilst I listen, as much as an epic has done before.   A dog drawn by a master, or a litter of pigs, satisfies, and is a reality not less than the frescos of Angelo.   From this succession of excellent objects learn we at last the immensity of the world, the opulence of human nature, which can run to infinitude in any direction.   But I also learn that what astonished and fascinated me in the first work astonished me in the second work also,—that excellence of all things is one.

   The office of painting and sculpture seems to be merely initial.   The best pictures can easily tell us their last secret.   The best pictures are rude draughts of a few of the miraculous dots and lines and dyes which make up the ever-changing " landscape with figures " amidst which we dwell.   Painting seems to be to the eye what dancing is to the limbs.   When that has educated the frame to self-possession, to nimbleness, to grace, the steps of the dancing master are better forgotten : so painting teaches me the splendour of colour and the expression of form, and as I see many pictures and higher genius in the art, I see the boundaries of opulence of the pencil, the indifferency in which the artist stands free to choose out of the possible forms.   If he can draw every thing, then why draw anything?   and then is my eye open to the eternal picture which natures paints in the street, with moving men and children, beggars and fine ladies, draped in red, and green, and blue, and grey ; long-haired, grizzled, white-faced, black-faced, wrinkled, giant, dwarf, expanded, elfish,—capped and based by heaven, earth, and sea.

A gallery of sculpture teaches me more austerely the same lesson. As picture teaches the colouring, so sculpture the anatomy of form. When I have seen fine statues, and afterwards enter a public assembly, I understand well what he meant who said, " When I have been reading Homer, all men look like giants."   I too see that painting and sculpture and gymnastics of the eye, its training to the niceties and curiosities of its function.   There is no statue like this living man, with his infinite advantage over all ideal sculpture, of perpetual variety. What a gallery of art have I here !   No mannerist made these varied groups and diverse original single figures.   Here is the artist himself improvising, grim and glad, at his block.   Now one thought strikes him, now another ; and with each moment he alters the whole air, attitude, and expression of his clay.   Away with your nonsense of oils and easels, of marble and chisels : except to open your eyes to the witchcraft of eternal art, they are hypocritical rubbish.

The reference of all production at last to an Aboriginal Power explains the traits common to all works of the highest art,—that they are universally intelligible, that they restore to us the simplest states of mind, and are religious. Since what skill is therein shown in reappearance of the original soul, a jet of pure light, it should produce a similar impression to that made by natural objects. In happy hours nature appears to us one with art ; art perfected, —the work of genius. And the individual in whom simple tastes, and susceptibility to all the great human influences, overpower the accidents of a local and special culture, is the best critic of art. Though we travel the world over to find the beautiful, we must carry it with us, or we find it not. The best of beauty is a finer charm than skill in surfaces, in outlines, or rules of art can ever teach, namely, a radiation, from the work of art, of human character, —a wonderful expression, through stone or canvas or musical sound, of the deepest and simplest attributes of our nature, and therefore most intelligible at last to those souls which have these attributes. In the sculptures of the Greeks, in the masonry of the Romans, and in the pictures of the Tuscan and Venetian masters, the highest charm is the universal language they speak. A confession of moral nature, of purity, love, and hope, breathes from them all. That which we carry to them, the same we bring back more fairly illustrated in the memory. The traveller who visits the Vatican, and passes from chamber to chamber through galleries of statues, vases, sarcophagi, and candelabra, through all forms of beauty, cut in the richest materials, is in danger of forgetting the simplicity of the principles out of which they all sprung, and that they had their origin from thoughts and laws in his own breast. He studies the technical rules on these wonderful remains, but forgets the these works were not always thus constellated ; that they are contributions of many ages and many countries ; that each came out of the solitary workshop of one artist, who toiled perhaps in ignorance of the existence of other sculpture, created his work without other model save life, household life, and the sweet and smart of personal relations, of beating hearts, and meeting eyes, of poverty, and necessity, and hope, and fear. These were his inspirations, and these are the effects he carries home to your heart and your mind. In proportion to his force, the artist will find his work an outlet for proper character. He must not be in any manner pinched or hindered by his material, but through his necessity of imparting himself, the adamant will be wax in his hands, and will allow an adequate communication of himself in his full stature and proportion. Not a conventional nature and culture need he cumber himself with, nor ask what is the mode in Rome or in Paris ; but that house, and weather, and manner of living, which poverty and the fate of birth have made at once so odious and so dear, in the grey unpainted wood cabin on the corner of a New Hampshire farm, or in the log-hut of the backwoods, or in the narrow lodging where he has endured the constraints and seeming of a city poverty, —will serve as well as any other condition as the symbol of a thought which pours itself indifferently through all.

I remember, when in my younger days I had heard of the wonders of Italian painting, I fancied the great pictures would be great strangers ; some surprising combination of colour and form ; a foreign wonder, barbaric pearl and gold, like the spontoons and standards of the militia, which play such pranks in the imagination of school-boys. I was to see and inquire I knew not what. When I came at last to Rome, and saw with eyes the pictures, I found that genius left to novices the gay and fantastic ostentatious, and itself pierced directly to the simple and true ; that it was familiar and sincere ; that it was the old eternal fact I had met already in so many forms ; unto which I lived ; that it was the plain *you and me* I know so well,—had left at home in so many conversations. I had the same experience already in a church at Naples. There I saw that nothing was changed with me but the place, and said to myself, —" Thou foolish child, hast thou come out hither, over four thousand miles of salt water, to find that which was perfect to thee there at home ? That fact I saw again in the Accademia at Naples, in the chambers of sculpture ; and yet again when I came to Rome, and to the paintings of Raphael, Angelo, Sacchi, Titian, and Leonardo da Vinci. " What, old mole ! workest thou in the earth so fast ?" It had travelled by my side : that which I fancied I had left in Boston was here in the Vatican, and again in Milan, and at Paris, and made all travelling ridiculous as a treadmill. I now require this of all pictures, that they domesticate me, not that they dazzle me. Pictures

must be too picturesque. Nothing astonishes men so much as
common sense and plain dealing. All great actions have been simple,
and all great pictures are.

The Transfiguration, by Raphael, is an eminent example of this
peculiar merit. A calm, benignant beauty shines over all this picture,
and goes directly to the heart. It seems almost to call you by name.
The sweet and sublime face of Jesus is beyond praise, yet how it
disappoints all florid expectations ! This familiar, simple, home-
speaking countenance is as if one should meet a friend. The
knowledge of pictures-dealers has its value ; but listen not to their
criticism when your heart is touched by genius. It was not painted for
them, —it was painted for you ; for such as had eyes capable of being
touched by simplicity and lofty emotions.

Yet when we have said all our fine things about the arts, we must
end with a frank confession, that the arts, as we know them, are but
initial. Our best praise is given to what they aimed and promised, not
to the actual result. He has conceived meanly of the resources of man
who believes that the best age of production is past. The real value of
the Iliad or the Transfiguration is as sings of power ; billows or ripples
they are of the great stream of tendency ; tokens of the everlasting
effort to produce, which even in its worst state the soul betrays. Art
has not yet come to its maturity, if it do not just itself abreast with the
most potent influences of the world, if it is not practical and moral, if it
do not stand in connexion with the conscience, if it do not make the
poor and uncultivated feel that it addresses them with a lofty cheer.
There is higher work for Art than the arts. They are abortive births of
an imperfect or vitiated instinct. Art is the need to create ; but in its
essence, immense and universal, it is impatient of working with lame
or tied hands, and of making cripples and monsters, such as all pictures
and statues are. Nothing less than the creation of man and nature is its
end. A man should find it an outlet for his whole energy. He may
paint and carve only as long as he can do that. Art should exhilarate,
and throw down the walls of circumstance on every side, awakening in

the beholder the same sense of universal relation and power which the work evinced in the artist, and its highest effect is to make new artists.

Already History is old enough to witness the old age and disappearance of particular arts. The art of sculpture is long ago perished to any real effect. It was originally an useful art, a mode of writing, a savage's record of gratitude or devotion ; and among a people possessed of a wonderful perception of from, this childish carving was refined to the utmost splendour of effect. But it is the game of a rude and youthful people, and not the manly labour of a wise and spiritual nation. Under an oak-tree loaded with leaves and nuts, under a sky full of eternal eyes, I stand in a thoroughfare ; but in the works of our plastic arts, and especially of sculpture, creation is driven into a corner. I cannot hide from myself that there is a certain appearance of paltriness, as of toys, and the trumpery of a theatre, in sculpture. Nature transcends all our moods of thought, and its secret we do not yet find. But the gallery stands at the mercy of our moods, and there is a moment when it becomes frivolous. I do not wonder that Newton, with an attention habitually engaged on the path of planets and suns, should have wondered what the Earl of Pembroke found to admire in " stone dolls." Sculpture may serve to teach the pupil how deep is the secret of form, how purely the sprit can translate its meanings into that eloquent dialect. But the statue will look cold and false before that new activity, which needs to roll through all things, and is impatient of counterfeits and things not alive. Picture and sculpture are the celebrations and festivities of form. But true art is never fixed, but always flowing. The sweetest music is not in the oratorio, but in the human voice when it speaks from its instant life tones of tenderness, truth, or courage. The oratorio has already lost its relation to the morning, to the sun and the earth, but that persuading voice is in tune with these. All works of art should not be detached, but extempore performances. A great man is a new statue in every attitude and action. A beautiful woman is a picture which drives all beholders nobly mad. Life may be lyric or epic, as well as a poem or a romance.

A true announcement of the law of creation, if a man were found worthy to declare it, would carry art up into the kingdom of nature, and destroy its separate and contrasted existence. The fountains of invention and beauty in modern society are all but dried up. A popular novel, a theatre, or a ball-room, makes us feel that we are all paupers in the alms-house of this world, without dignity, without skill or industry. Art is as poor and low. The old tragic Necessity, which lowers on the brows even of the Venuses and the Cupids of the antique, and furnishes the sole apology for the intrusion of such anomalous figures into nature, —namely, they they were inevitable, that the artist was drunk with a passion for form, which he could not resist, and which vented itself in these fine extravagances, —no longer dignifies the chisel or the pencil. But the artist and the connoisseur now seek in the art the exhibition of their talent, or an asylum from the evils of life. Men are not well pleased with the figure they make in their own imagination, and they flee to art, and convey their better sense in an oratorio, a statue, or a picture. Art makes the same effort which a sensual prosperity makes, namely, to detach the beautiful from the useful, to do up the work as unavoidable, and hating it, pass on to enjoyment. These solaces and compensations, this division of beauty from use, the laws of nature do not permit. As soon as beauty is sought not from religion and love, but for pleasure, it degrades the seeker. High beauty is no longer attainable by him in canvas or stone, in sound or in lyrical construction ; an effeminate, prudent, sickly beauty, which is not beauty, is all that can be formed ; for the hand can never execute anything higher than the character can inspire.

The art that thus separates is itself first separated. Art must not be a superficial talent, but must begin farther back in man. Now men do not see nature to be beautiful, and they go to make a statue which shall be. They abhor men as tasteless, dull, and inconvertible, and console themselves with colour-bags and blocks of marble. They reject life as prosaic, and create a death which they call poetic. They dispatch the day's weary chores, and fly to voluptuous reveries. They eat and drink, that they may afterwards execute the ideal. This is art vilified ;

the name conveys to the mind its secondary and bad senses ; it stands in the imagination as somewhat contrary to nature, and struck with death from the first. Would it not be better to begin higher up, —to serve the ideal before they eat and drink ; to serve the ideal in eating and drinking, in drawing the breath, and in the functions of life ? Beauty must come back to the useful arts, and the distinction between the fine and the useful arts be forgotten. If history were truly told, if life were nobly spent, it would be no longer easy or possible to distinguish one from the other. It nature all is useful, all is beautiful. It is therefore beautiful because it is alive, moving, reproductive ; it is therefore useful because it is symmetrical and fair. Beauty will not come at the call of a legislature, nor will it repeat in England or America its history in Greece. It will come, as always, unannounced, and spring up between the feet of brave and earnest men. It is in vain that we look for genius to reiterate its miracles in the old arts ; it is its instinct to find beauty and holiness in new and necessary facts, in the field and roadside, in the shop and mill. Proceeding from a religious heart, it will raise to a divine use the railroad, the insurance-office, the joint-stock company, our law, our primary assemblies, our commerce, the galvanic battery, the electric jar, the prism, and the chemist's retort, in which we seek now only an economical use. Is not the selfish and even cruel aspect which belongs to our great mechanical works, to mills, railways, and machinery, the effect of the mercenary impulses which these works obey ? When its errands are noble and adequate, a steam-boat bridging the Atlantic between Old and New England, and arriving as its ports with the punctuality of a planet, —is a step of a man into harmony with nature. The boat at St Petersburg, which plies along the Lena by magnetism, needs little to make it sublime. When science is learned in love, and its powers are wielded by love, they will appear the supplements and continuations of the material creation.

Made in the USA
Monee, IL
28 May 2023

34799553R00122